Clever with Lamb

HOME COOKING

© 1994 Time-Life Books B.V.
First published jointly by Time-Life Books B.V. and
Geddes & Grosset Ltd.

Material in this book was first published as part of the series
HEALTHY HOME COOKING.

ISBN 0 7054 2032 9

Printed in Italy.

Clever with Lamb

BY
THE EDITORS OF TIME-LIFE BOOKS

TIME-LIFE/GEDDES & GROSSET

Contents

A New approach to Lamb

Over the millennia no meat has more regularly graced the tables of mankind than lamb. It was some 10,000 years ago that tribesmen in Central Asia first domesticated sheep for their meat, milk and wool. By 7,000 B C the pastoral way of life had become widespread throughout the Middle East, where flocks of hardy sheep thrived despite punishing extremes of heat and cold. Little wonder that sheep are the first domestic animal mentioned in the Bible. Adam's son Abel, we learn in Genesis, was 'a keeper of sheep', and when he made a sacrifice to God, he chose to offer up his new-born lambs.

During its association with mankind, the sheep has evenhandedly fed both the rich and the poor. In many parts of the world its meat has long been served for feasting and holy days, but equally for everyday fare. In medieval Europe, the servant who carried the roast saddle of lamb, crisp and golden, to the banqueting table, returned to the kitchen for his own bowl of mutton stew—not such an imposing dish as his master's but just as nutritious and full of flavour. Throughout the Islamic Middle East, a whole roast lamb is still the centrepiece of wedding feasts and other festivities, while lesser cuts play a central role in most ordinary meat dishes.

In other parts of the prosperous modern world, however, this most democratic of providers has lost its pride of place in many kitchens. Beef and pork, as well as poultry such as chicken, are today all produced inexpensively enough to compete with lamb at the table. A further blow to the prestige of lamb comes from health-conscious cooks who are wary of the fat content of red meats in general, and who regard lamb as having only a limited place in a healthy diet.

This volume aims to restore lamb to its rightful place as a food for everyman. Reflecting its classless appeal, the 55 recipes offer inspiration for every kind of occasion, summer or winter. There are simple chops and cutlets, grand roasts, subtly avoured stews, assemblages of meat and vegetables, sautés and salads. Devised by Time-Life Books' own team of chefs and nutritionists, these dishes have been prepared with a minimum of fat and oil, allowing the most health-conscious cooks to choose freely from among them.

A nutritional profile

By any standards, lamb, like other red meats, is a highly nutritious, food. A single 90 g (3 oz) serving of cooked lamb provides about 20 g (^{3}/$_4$ oz) of valuable animal protein—one third of the total daily intake recommended for adults. Just as beneficial is the range of vitamins present in red meat. Lamb is an important source of B vitamins, essential for a healthy skin and nervous system. A 90 g (3 oz) serving, for example, contains over 40 per cent of the adult male's recommended daily intake of niacin and of vitamin B12. Lamb is also rich in iron, in the form known as 'haem iron', which is not only easily absorbed by the body, but also promotes the absorption of iron from other foods.

The major drawback of lamb as part of a healthy diet is its high fat content. Most people are aware that we eat too much fat for our own well-being. Indeed, nutritionists urge us to cut our total fat consumption by about one quarter—from nearly 40 per cent of our daily energy intake to about 30 per cent. They are especially insistent on the wisdom of cutting down on saturated fats—contained in animal fats— which promote the production of cholesterol in the body. Although cholesterol is produced naturally by the liver and in small amounts contributes to good health, excessive production stimulated by a diet high in saturated fats can, over a period of time, lead to heart disease.

Fortunately, lamb is a less fatty meat than it used to be. European farmers, encouraged by consumer demand and, in the U.K., by agricultural subsidies, are generally producing leaner lamb than was available a few years ago. In any case, most of the fat found in a cut of lamb can easily be trimmed off before cooking. But lean, uncooked lamb still contains about 9 per cent intramuscular fat. This proportion is slightly higher than is found in pork, and about twice as much as is present lean beef. In other words, a certain intake of satuated fat cannot be avoided when you sit down to a dish of lamb. You would not want it otherwise, for fat in reasonable measure contributes to the flavour and succulence of meat; it is one of the reasons why lamb has been so highly regarded for so long.

The healthy strategy adopted by the authors of this volume is to prepare the meat so that it is as fat-free as possible, and to eliminate all unnecessary fats from the cooking process, using the much more benign polyunsaturated or monounsaturated fats where necessary. An upper limit of 14 g total fat per 90 g (3 oz) serving of cooked lamb has been imposed as a reasonable guideline. These recipes also limit salt to no more than 400 mg per portion, since a high salt intake is also implicated in heart disease. At the same time, Time-Life Books' team of cooks and nutrition experts have in no way compromised the unique flavour and texture of lamb.

Choosing, buying and storing

A recommended first step in buying good-quality lean lamb is to seek the advice of a knowledgeable butcher. He should be able to tell you the age and origin of the animal—factors that influence the appearance, flavour and fat content of the meat. As a general rule, the younger the lamb the paler and less fatty the meat. Lowland breeds are not inherently leaner than hill breeds, but they gain weight faster and are usually slaughtered at an earlier age. A fresh spring lamb of about six months has rosepink flesh and white, firm fat; brittle, chalk-white fat suggests that the meat has been frozen. Certain hill breeds, however, have darker flesh than lowland strains, as does meat that has been hung. A useful indicator of a lamb's age is its bones; in a young animal they have a pinkish-blue tinge, while in older animals they are white and less pliant.

There is no general agreement as to when lamb becomes mutton, for different breeds mature at different rates. It is safe to say, however, that an animal is no longer sold as lamb after it is a year old. Of course, mutton is now something of a rarity in Europe, being found mainly in butcher's shops which cater for Asian or Middle Eastern communities.

Although the emphasis in this volume is on lean cuts, the recipes also make use of cuts from most other parts of the carcass. Not included are recipes for the breast and the middle and scrag end of neck (the section nearest the head), which have a very high fat content, even after trimming. The liver, although a rich source of vitamin A, has a cholesterol content that exceeds the limit prescribed for healthy diets, and should only be eaten occasionally. Shoulder of lamb appears infrequently in the recipes; full of flavour but also high in fat, this cut requires meticulous trimming before it is cooked.

The principal source of lean meat on a lamb is the fillet end—the wide upper section—of the leg. Cuts from the fillet can be cubed for stews and kebabs, minced for meat loaf and kofta, or sliced and pounded flat to create lamb's answer to the veal escalope, ideal for quick grilling or flash-frying. The best end of neck and the loin—adjacent cuts along the back of the carcass—yield smaller pieces of extremely tender lean meat. The best end, whether roasted whole as a rack or separated into individual cutlets, should be carefully trimmed of fat so that only the 'eye' of lean meat along the backbone remains. Likewise, the loin can be cut into chops and trimmed of fat, or boned to yield two strips of lean meat—the eye and the small but exquisitely tender fillet.

Several of the preparatory techniques are tasks routinely undertaken by a butcher, whose work is time-saving and usually free. You can order ready-to-cook noisettes, for example, or a boned leg or loin. Alternatively, buy the basic cuts and prepare them for cooking yourself; no doubt your own efforts will be slow, but you can take satisfaction in removing every piece of surplus fat. Likewise, the leanest and freshest mince is obtained by chopping by hand at home.

Stored in the coolest part of the refrigerator, fresh lamb will keep without spoiling for up to three days. Remove its wrapping and place it on a rack above a plate to encourage the circulation of air. Cover it with an upturned bowl to prevent its surface from drying out. Minced lamb, however, should be eaten within two days of being refrigerated.

Lamb will keep in the freezer for six to nine months; minced lamb for four months. Freeze only fresh meat, extracting all air from the freezer bag or foil parcel before storing.

Appetizing flavours, healthy techniques

To keep fat and cholesterol levels within healthy limits the recipes that follow call for skimmed milk in place of whole milk and polyunsaturated margarine rather than butter. Cheese is used only as a topping, never a principal ingredient, while cream—that staple of the traditional rich sauce—finds sumptuous but relatively low-fat replacement in thick Greek yoghurt. To reduce both fat and calories, gravies and sauces are thickened with cornflour or arrowroot, rarely with the traditional roux made from plain flour and fat.

Far from limiting the variety and appeal of the recipes, these restrictions free a range of flavours that too

The Key to Better Eating

Home Cooking addresses the concerns of today's weight-conscious, health-minded cooks with recipes that take into account guidelines set by nutritionists. The secret of eating well, of course, has to do with maintaining a balance of foods in the diet. The recipes thus should be used thoughtfully, in the context of a day's eating. To make the choice easier, an analysis is given of nutrients in a single serving. The counts for calories, protein, cholesterol, total fat, saturated fat, and sodium are approximate.

Interpreting the chart

The chart below gives dietary guidelines for healthy men, women and children. Recommended figures vary from country to country, but the principles are the same everywhere. The average daily amounts of calories and protein are from a report by the UK Department of Health and Social Security; the maximum advisable daily intake of fat is based on guidelines given by the National Advisory Committee on Nutrition Education (NACNE); those for cholesterol and sodium are based on upper limits suggested by the World Health Organization.

The volumes in the Home Cooking series do not purport to be diet books, nor do they focus on health foods. Rather, they express a common-sense approach to cooking that uses salt, sugar, cream, butter and oil in moderation, while employing other ingredients that also provide flavour and satisfaction. The portions themselves are modest in size.

The recipes make few unusual demands. Naturally they call for fresh ingredients, offering substitutes when these are unavailable. (The substitute is not calculated in the nutrient analysis, however.) Most of the ingredients can be found in any well-stocked supermarket.

Heavy-bottomed pots and pans are recommended to guard against burning whenever a small amount of oil is used and where there is danger of the food adhering to the hot surface, but non-stick pans can be utilized as well. Both safflower oil and virgin olive oil are favoured for sautéing. Safflower oil was chosen because it is the most highly polyunsaturated vegetable fat available in supermarkets, and polyunsaturated fats reduce blood cholesterol; if unobtainable, use sunflower oil, also high in polyunsaturated fats. Virgin olive oil is used because it has a fine fruity flavour lacking in the lesser grade known as 'pure'. In addition, it is—like all olive oil—high in monounsaturated fats, which are thought not to increase blood cholesterol. When virgin olive oil is unavailable, or when its flavour is not essential to the success of the dish, 'pure' may be used.

About cooking times

To help planning, time is taken into account in the recipes. While recognizing that everyone cooks at a different speed and that stoves and ovens differ, approximate 'working' and 'total' times are provided. Working time stands for the minutes actively spent on preparation; total time includes unattended cooking time, as well as time devoted to marinating, steeping or soaking ingredients. Since the recipes emphasize fresh foods, they may take a bit longer to prepare than 'quick and easy' dishes that call for canned or packaged products, but the difference in flavour, and often in nutrition, should compensate for the little extra time involved.

Recommended Dietary Guidelines

Average Daily Intake				Maximum Daily Intake			
		Calories	Protein *grams*	Cholesterol *milligrams*	Total fat *grams*	Saturated fat *grams*	Sodium *milligrams*
Females	7-8	1900	47	300	80	32	2000*
	9-11	2050	51	300	77	35	2000
	12-17	2150	53	300	81	36	2000
	18-54	2150	54	300	81	36	2000
	55-74	1900	47	300	72	32	2000
Males	7-8	1980	49	300	80	33	2000
	9-11	2280	57	300	77	38	2000
	12-14	2640	66	300	99	44	2000
	15-17	2880	72	300	108	48	2000
	18-34	2900	72	300	109	48	2000
	35-64	2750	69	300	104	35	2000
	65-74	2400	60	300	91	40	2000

* *(or 5 g salt)*

often are suppressed by rich ingredients. Fibre-rich fresh vegetables and grains, dried fruits and pulses are traditional partners for lamb, and they a made full use of here. The reduced level of salt permits fresh herbs and spices to assert their flavours with refreshing clarity.

Cooking techniques are also tailored to meet the dietary guidelines. Heavy bottomed pans used to guard against burning the food when a small amount of oil is used. But non-stick pans brushed with the merest film oil are perfectly adequate for browning meat and vegetables, as called for in many of the recipes. Safflower oil and virgin olive oil sautéing. Safflower oil has been chosen because it is the most highly polyunsaturated oil generally available—and polyunsaturated vegetable fats are not only blameless in the cholesterol controversy, but may actually reduce the blood cholesterool evel. A good second choice is sunflower oil, also high in polyunsaturated fats. Virgin olive oil is called for because it has matches fruity flavour and—like all olive oil—is high in monounsaturated fats, which are not nked to increased blood cholesterol levels. Lesser grades olive oil, such 'pure', can be substituted for 'virgin', though they lack its incomparable bouquet.

When cooked slowly in a liquid, even the leanest of amb will release a small amount of fat. If the cooking liquid is to be used for a sauce or gravy, skim off the at with a ladle or shallow spoon before serving. Alternatively, lay a paper towel flat on the surface, then lift it away immediately it has absorbed the layer of fat. A stew that is prepared in advance of a meal can be chilled and then degreased even more thoroughly simply by lifting off the solid layer of fat that collects at the surface.

Keeping low-fat cuts of meat moist is a particular probelm when sautéeing, grilling or roasting. Denied the traditional techniques of basting or ladling the meat with extra fat, the health-conscious cook must adopt different strategies. One such method is to stuff a roast or chop with a savoury filling that moisturizes the meat from within as it cooks. Another technique, suitable for thin cuts of lamb, is to tenderize the meat in a marinade so that it cooks rapidly with a minimum wastage of moisture. Acidic marinades, made with vinegar, wine or citrus juices blended with aromatics, will break down the meat's fibres while imparting their own flavours. Treated in this way, a slice of fillet end of leg flattened with a meat bat will grill in very little time under a searing heat—and will taste all the better for the marriage of flavours.

Whatever techniques you use to keep lamb moist, prolonged exposure to dry heat will eventually desiccate the meat. For this reason, the range of cooking times recommended in the recipes are for rare to medium meat. If lamb that is still pink in the middle is not to your taste, add a minute or two to the cooking time for small pieces and 10 to 15 minutes for joints.

A choice of cooking methods.

The ingredient list for each recipe starts with lamb and continues with the other ingredients in order of use. Both metric and imperial weights and volumes are given; the two sets of figures are not exact equivalents and should not be used together.

Like other volumes in this series, Clever with Lamb presents an analysis of nutrients contained in a single serving, plus approximate counts for calories, protein, cholesterol, total fat, saturated fat and sodium.

Medallions with Watercress Sauce

Serves 4

Working time: about 35 minutes

Total time: about 45 minutes

Calories 200, Protein 25g, Cholesterol 90mg,
Total fat 11g, Saturated fat 5g, Sodium 90mg

1 kg/2¼ lb	loin of lamb, boned, trimmed of fat, eye cut diagonally into 12 slices, fillet reserved for another use
30 cl/½ pint	unsalted brown or chicken stock
2	bunches watercress, washed
4	fresh sage leaves, or ⅛ tsp dried sage
½ tsp	salt
	white pepper
1 tbsp	apple jelly
1 tbsp	Worcester sauce, mixed with 1 tbsp water
1 tbsp	fromage frais

To make the watercress sauce, boil the stock until the liquid is reduced by half—5 to 10 minutes. Strip the leaves from the watercress, reserving four sprigs for garnish, and add the watercress and sage leaves to the reduced boiling stock. Cook the stock for a further 1 minute, allow it to cool slightly, then purée it in a blender or food processor. Transfer it to a small pan, season with half of the salt and some pepper and add the apple jelly. Stir the sauce over low heat until the jelly has melted, then remove the pan from the heat.

Season the lamb slices with the remaining ¼ teaspoon of salt and some pepper. Lightly brush a large non-stick frying pan with oil and brown six of the slices over high heat for 1 minute on each side. Reduce the heat to medium, add half of the Worcester sauce mixture and cook for a further 30 seconds to 1 minute on each side for rare to medium meat. Transfer the meat to a platter and keep it warm. Cook the remaining slices in the same way.

Heat the watercress sauce through, then remove it from the heat and stir in the *fromage frais*. Serve the lamb with the sauce, garnished with the reserved sprigs of watercress.

Flambéed Cutlets with Stuffed Apricots

Serves 4

Working time about 40 minutes

Total time: about 6 hours and 50 minutes
(includes soaking and marinating)

Calories 260, Protein 31g, Cholesterol 75mg, Total fat 8g,
Saturated fat 4g, Sodium 175mg

8	*best end of neck cutlets (about 90 g/3 oz each), trimmed of fat*
2 tbsp	*coarsely chopped fresh ginger root*
2	*garlic cloves, coarsely chopped*
1	*small onion, coarsely chopped*
15 cl/¹/₄ pint	*fresh orange juice*
¹/₄ tsp	*virgin olive oil*
125 g/4 oz	*mushrooms, finely chopped*
¹/₄ tsp	*salt*
	freshly ground black pepper
8	*dried whole apricots, soaked in water for 6 hours, or overnight*
2 tbsp	*brandy*
	parsley, for garnish (optional)

ace the cutlets in a single layer in a shallow dish or
asserole. Blend together the ginger, garlic, half the
hopped onion and the orange juice in a food proces-
or. Spoon the purée over the cutlets, cover loosely

and leave them to marinate for at least 6 hours, or
overnight, turning them once.

Heat the oil in a heavy frying pan. Add the mushrooms and the remaining onion, season them with half
the salt and some pepper and sauté over medium heat
until they are soft—2 to 3 minutes.

Dry the apricots on paper towels and fill them with
the mushroom and onion stuffing, enlarging the hole
from which the stone was removed if necessary.

Remove the cutlets from the marinade and pat them
dry with paper towels, strain the marinade and reserve
it. Preheat a non-stick sauté pan and sear the cutlets
for 1 minute on each side. Add the brandy and light it
with a taper. When the flame dies down, arrange the
stuffed apricots in the pan, pour in half of the marinade and sprinkle with the remaining salt. Cover with
a tight fitting lid and cook over low heat until the juices
are still slightly pink when the cutlet is pierced with a
knife—about 10 minutes.

Arrange the meat and stuffed apricots on a warm
platter. Skim off any fat from the juices in the pan,
then add the remaining marinade, bring it to the boil
and simmer for 1 minute. Spoon the sauce over the
lamb and serve, garnished, if you like, with parsley.

Medallions in Sweet-and-Sour Sauce

Serves 4

Working (and total) time: about 40 minutes

Calories 305, Protein 26g, Cholesterol 85mg,
Total fat 14g, Saturated fat 6g, Sodium 165mg

1	rack of lamb(about 850 g/1³/4 lb), boned, the fatty flap of meat that extends from the eye removed
20	shallots
20 g/³/4 oz	unsalted butter
2 tbsp	red wine
2 tsp	clear honey
¹/2 tsp	salt
	freshly ground black pepper
	chopped spring onions, for garnish

Sweet-and-sour sauce

200 g/7 oz	young carrots
200 g/7 oz	young pink rhubarb
10 cm/4 inch	piece fresh ginger root
¹/4 litre/8 fl oz	red wine
4 tbsp	finely chopped shallots
60 cl/1 pint	unsalted brown stock
1 tsp	clear honey

Start by preparing the ingredients for the sauce. Cut half the carrots and rhubarb into 6 cm by 3 mm (2¹/2 by ¹/8 inch) sticks. Chop the remainder coarsely. Cut half the ginger into matchsticks, and finely chop the rest. Blanch the carrot sticks in boiling water for 1 minute, refresh them immediately in cold water and drain.

Preheat the oven to 130°C (250°F or Mark ¹/2). Put 15 g (¹/2 oz) of the butter in a heavy frying pan and sauté the whole shallots over medium heat until they begin to soften and turn golden-brown—4 to 5 minutes. Pour in the 2 tablespoons of wine and the honey, increase the heat and boil, stirring frequently, until the liquid reduces to a syrupy glaze. Place the shallots in a roasting pan in the oven.

Cut the lamb across the grain into 16 medallions. Season them with the salt and freshly ground pepper.

Melt the remaining butter in a heavy frying pan over low heat. Sauté the ginger matchsticks for 2 to 3 seconds, add the carrot sticks and sauté them for 10 seconds, then add the rhubarb sticks and sauté all the ingredients for a further 10 seconds, stirring all the time. Remove the sticks with a slotted spoon, transfer them to a plate, cover them and keep warm.

Increase the heat to high and brown the medallions for 1 to 2 minutes on each side. Put them in the roasting pan in the oven with the glazed shallots.

To finish making the sauce, pour off any fat from the frying pan. Put the pan over high heat, pour in the red wine and bring it to the boil, stirring to dislodge any meat deposits. Add the chopped shallots together with the chopped ginger, carrots and rhubarb. Boil until only half the liquid remains, then add the stock and the honey and continue boiling until the liquid is reduced by half again. Strain the sauce through a fine sieve into a clean saucepan. Add the carrot and rhubarb sticks and the ginger matchsticks and heat through.

Place four medallions on each of four warmed plates, pour the sauce round them and garnish with the spring onions. Serve with the glazed shallots.

Lamb and Broccoli Stir-Fry

Serves 4
Working (and total) time: about 25 minutes
Calories 245, Protein 22g, Cholesterol 50mg, Total fat 8g,
Saturated fat 3g, Sodium 270mg

350 g/12 oz	*lean lamb (from the loin), cut into thin strips*
4 tsp	*safflower oil*
20 g/³/₄ oz	*fermented black beans, soaked in water for 5 minutes*
¹/₂ tsp	*sesame oil*
1	*onion, halved lengthwise, cut into strips*
2	*garlic cloves, finely chopped*
2.5 cm/1 inch	*piece fresh ginger root, finely chopped*
175 g/6 oz	*broccoli, blanched, stalks peeled and julienned, flowers divided into florets*
2	*sticks celery, chopped*
1	*sweet red pepper, seeded, deribbed and thinly sliced*
1 tsp	*low-sodium soy sauce or shoyu*
200 g/7 oz	*fresh water chestnuts, peeled and boiled for 3 minutes, or canned water chestnuts drained*
3 tbsp	*medium sherry*

Heat 1 teaspoon of the safflower oil in a wok or a large heavy frying pan and stir-fry half of the lamb over a medium heat, tossing and stirring until it is browned— about 2 minutes. Remove the lamb from the wok and keep it warm. Heat another teaspoon of the oil in the wok, stir-fry the remaining meat and add it to the first batch.

Drain the black beans and mash them in a small bowl with the sesame oil to make a coarse paste. Set aside. Put the remaining safflower oil into the wok or frying pan, add the onion, chopped garlic and ginger and stir-fry for 1 minute. Add the broccoli, celery, red pepper and soy sauce and stir-fry for a further 2 minutes. Add the water chestnuts, black bean paste and sherry, and return the lamb to the wok. Stir-fry over medium heat for a further 2 minutes, so that all the ingredients are coated with the sauce and heated through. Serve immediately.

Lamb Medallions on Courgette Pancakes

Serves 1

Working and total time: about 30 minutes

Calories 235, Protein 26g, Cholesterol 70mg, Total fat 9g,
Saturated fat 4g, Sodium 295mg

1 kg/2¹/₄ lb	*loin, boned and trimmed of fat eye only*
3 tbsp	*cut chives or finely chopped spring onions, for garnish*

Courgette pancakes

350 g/12 oz	*courgettes grated*
1	*carrot, grated*
1	*egg white*
3 tbsp	*freshly grated Parmesan cheese*
2 tbsp	*wholemeal flour*
2	*garlic cloves, finely chopped*
¹/₄ tsp	*salt*
	freshly ground black pepper
1 tsp	*safflower oil*

Cut the eye of into eight slices. With a meat bat or the flat of a heavy knife pound each slice between plastic film or greaseproof paper to a thickness of about 5 mm (¹/₄ inch). Set the medallions aside.

Combine all the pancake ingredients except the oil in a bowl and mix them well.

Heat a large, non-stick frying pan over medium heat. Add the oil and spread it over the bottom with a paper towel. Drop four 2 tablespoon mounds of the pancake mixture into the pan, allowing ample room between them. With a spatula, spread out each mound to form a pancake about 7.5 cm (3 inches) in diameter. Cook the pancakes until they are lightly browned—about 3 minutes on each side. Transfer the pancakes to a baking sheet and keep them warm in a very low oven. Cook four more pancakes in the same way.

Increase the heat under the pan to high. Add the medallions to the pan and cook them until they are browned about 2 minutes oil each side.

Put two courgette pancakes on each of four plates, top each pancake with a lamb medallion. Sprinkle the medallions with the cut chives or chopped spring onions, and serve at once.

EDITOR'S NOTE: Only the eye of the loin is used here, reserve the fillet for another recopie where lean meat is called for.

Peppered Steaks with Bean Sprout Salad

Serves 4

Working (and total) time: about 40 minutes

Calories 260, Protein 28g, Cholesterol 80mg,
Total fat 12g, Saturated fat 4g, Sodium 330mg

4	boned steaks (about 140 g/4¹/₂ oz each), cut from the fillet end of the leg, trimmed of fat
2 tsp	black peppercorns
¹/₄ tsp	salt
1 tbsp	virgin olive oil
3 tbsp	brandy
30 cl/¹/₂ pint	unsalted chicken stock
1 tbsp	cornflour
	celery leaves, for garnish

Bean sprout salad

2 tsp	Dijon mustard
¹/₂	lemon, juice only
3 tbsp	thick Greek yoghurt
1 tbsp	chopped parsley
¹/₄ tsp	salt
	freshly ground black pepper
175 g/6 oz	bean sprouts, rinsed and drained well
10 cm/4 inch	piece cucumber, julienned
3	sticks celery, chopped
1	small sweet red pepper, seeded, deribbed and thinly sliced

First prepare the salad. Put the mustard, lemon juice, yoghurt and parsley into a salad bowl, season with the salt and some pepper, and mix well together. Add the bean sprouts, cucumber, celery and red pepper. Stir all the salad ingredients thoroughly, then cover the bowl and refrigerate while cooking the steaks.

Crush the peppercorns coarsely using a mortar and pestle. Cut each steak into two neat pieces, then coat them on both sides with the crushed peppercorns and season with the salt.

Heat the olive oil over medium heat in a large, heavy frying pan. Add the steaks and cook them for 3 to 4 minutes on each side for rare to medium meat. Using a slotted spoon, transfer the steaks to a hot serving dish. Cover them and keep them hot.

Skim off any fat from the frying pan. Pour in the brandy, heat it for a few seconds, then ignite it using a taper. As soon as the flame subsides, add the stock and bring the liquid to the boil, stirring and scraping the sediment from the bottom of the pan into the sauce. In a small bowl, blend the cornflour with 1 tablespoon of cold water, then stir it into the sauce. Bring the sauce to the boil, reduce the heat and simmer for 2 to 3 minutes, stirring frequently, until the sauce thickens.

Strain the sauce over and round the peppered steaks. Garnish them with the celery leaves and serve immediately, accompanied by the bean sprout salad.

Loin and Liver Cassis

Serves 4

Working time: about 30 minutes

Total time: about 40 minutes

Calories 175, Protein 18g, Cholesterol 105mg,
Total fat 8g, Saturated fat 3g, Sodium 35mg

300 g/10 oz	lean lamb (from the loin) trimmed of fat, thinly sliced and flattened to about 3 mm (¹/₈ inch) thick
60 g/2 oz	lamb's liver, very thinly sliced
12	shallots
7 g/¹/₄ oz	unsalted butter
2 tbsp	plus 1 tsp crème de cassis
1¹/₂ tsp	blackcurrant or red wine vinegar
³/₄ tsp	salt
15cl/¹/₄ pint	unsalted chicken stock
2 tsp	plain flour
	freshly ground black pepper

Place the shallots in a small, heavy-bottomed, non-reactive saucepan with the butter, the teaspoon of crème de cassis, ¹/₂ teaspoon of the vinegar, ¹/₄ teaspoon of the salt and 3 tablespoons of water. Cover tightly, bring to the boil and simmer until the shallots are tender—about 25 minutes. Remove the lid, increase the heat

and boil off the residual liquid to glaze the shallots, shaking the pan occasionally to prevent them from burning. Set the shallots aside and keep them warm.

Meanwhile, pour the stock and the remaining crème de cassis into a separate non-reactive saucepan. Boil it rapidly until the liquid has reduced by about one half—5 to 10 minutes. Set the reduced stock aside.

Sift the flour with some pepper and toss the liver in the seasoned flour until it is evenly coated. Brush a large, heavy frying pan lightly with oil, place it over very high heat and sear the slices of loin for 20 to 30 seconds on each side. Transfer them to a heated serving dish, sprinkle them with pepper and keep them warm. Reduce the heat to low, brush the pan with a little more oil and cook the floured slices of liver for 20 to 30 seconds, stirring constantly. Remove the liver and set it aside.

Increase the heat under the pan and add the remaining teaspoon of vinegar. Allow it to bubble for a few seconds, then add the reduced stock and the remaining ¹/₂ teaspoon of salt. Bring to the boil, return the liver to the pan and simmer for a further 30 seconds before spooning the sauce and liver over the slices of loin. Serve with the glazed shallots.

Kasha-Coated Lamb with Parsley-Garlic Sauce

Serves 4

Working (and total time): about 20 minutes)

Calories 410, Protein 35g, Cholesterol 85mg,
Total fat 14g, Saturated fat 5g, Sodium 75mg

4	lamb slices (about 125g/ ^{1}/$_4$ oz each), cut from the fillet end of the leg, trimmed of fat and flattened to about 5 mm (^{1}/$_4$ inch) thick
1	egg white
1 tbsp	fresh lemon juice
200 g/7 oz	toasted buckwheat groats (kasha)
^{1}/$_4$ tsp	salt
	freshly ground black pepper
1 tbsp	virgin olive oil
^{1}/$_2$ tbsp	unsalted butter
1	shallot, finely chopped
1	garlic clove, finely chopped
60 g/2 oz	parsley, chopped
1	large ripe tomato, skinned, seeded and puréed in a food processor or blender

In a shallow bowl, whisk together the egg white and lemon juice. Spread the buckwheat groats on a plate. Sprinkle the lamb slices with the salt and some pepper. Dip a slice in the egg white mixture, then dredge it in the buckwheat groats, coating both sides. Repeat the process to coat the remaining slices of lamb.

Heat the oil and butter in a large, heavy or non-stick frying pan over high heat. Add the coated lamb slices and cook them until they are lightly browned on one side—about 3 minutes. Turn the slices and cook them for 2 minutes more to brown the second side. Transfer the slices to a warmed platter.

Add the chopped shallot, garlic and parsley to the pan and cook them for 1 minute. Stir in the puréed tomato and a generous grinding of black pepper. Cook the mixture for 1 minute more, then pour it over the lamb slices. Serve immediately.

17

Lamb with Aubergine and Parmesan

Serves 4

Working time: about 40 minutes

Total time: about 1 hour

Calories 450, Protein 34g, Cholesterol 80mg,
Total fat 10g, Saturated fat 4g, Sodium 235mg

500 g/1 lb	*lean lamb (from the leg or loin), trimmed of fat and cut into 1 cm (¹/₄ inch) pieces*
250 g/8 oz	*pasta shells*
1 tsp	*virgin olive oil*
250 g/8 oz	*pearl onions, blanched in boiling water for 2 minutes and peeled*
250 g/8 oz	*small mushrooms wiped clean*
350 g/12 oz	*aubergine, cut into 1 cm (¹/₂ inch) cubes*
1 tsp	*fresh thyme, or ¹/₂ tsp dried thyme*
	freshly ground black pepper
15g/¹/₂ oz	*Parmesan cheese, shaved with a vegetable peeler or grated*

Add the pasta to 3 litres (5 pints) of boiling water with 1¹/₂ teaspoons of salt. Start testing the pasta for doneness after 6 minutes and cook it until it is *al dente*. Drain the pasta, rinse it under cold running water to prevent the shells from sticking together and set aside while you cook the meat and vegetables.

Heat a large, non-stick sauté pan over high heat. Add the pieces of lamb and sauté them until they are browned on all sides—about 3 minutes. Reduce the heat to medium and cook the lamb for 3 minutes more. Remove the meat from the pan and set it aside.

Add the olive oil and onions to the sauté pan. Cover the pan and cook the onions, stirring occasionally, until they are browned—about 15 minutes. Add the mushrooms and aubergine cubes, then increase the heat to high, and sauté the vegetables until all of them are browned and the mushrooms and aubergine are soft—6 to 8 minutes.

Return the lamb to the pan; add the pasta, the thyme and a generous grinding of pepper. Sauté the mixture until the pasta is heated through—about 3 minutes. Spoon the mixture into a warmed serving dish and top it with the cheese. Serve immediately.

Lamb Paprika

Serves 4

Working time: about 25 minutes

Total time: about 6 hours and 25 minutes
(includes marinating)

Calories 245, Protein 30g, Cholesterol 85mg,
Total fat 11g, Saturated fat 5g, Sodium 350mg

500 g/1 lb	lean lamb (from the fillet end of the leg), trimmed of fat and cut into thin strips
1 tbsp	paprika
1/4 tsp	freshly ground black pepper
1/2 tsp	salt
350 g/12 oz	kale, washed, stemmed and chopped
2 tsp	caraway seeds
15 g/1/2 oz	polyunsaturated margarine
1	garlic clove, crushed
3	shallots, thinly sliced
2	bay leaves
3	tomatoes, skinned and chopped
3 tbsp	medium-dry sherry
2 tbsp	soured cream

ut the lamb in a bowl with the paprika, the pepper and half of the salt, and stir until the meat is evenly coated. Cover the bowl and leave it in a cool place to marinate for at least 6 hours or overnight. Stir the meat once during this period.

Pour enough water into a large saucepan to fill it about 2.5 cm (1 inch) deep. Place a vegetable steamer in the pan and bring the water to the boil. Put the chopped kale in the steamer and sprinkle it with the remaining salt and the caraway seeds. Cover the saucepan and cook until the kale is just tender and bright green—5 to 6 minutes.

Meanwhile, melt the margarine in a large, heavy frying pan. Stir in the garlic, shallots and bay leaves and cook them over medium heat until the shallots are softened—1 to 2 minutes. Increase the heat to high and sauté the lamb, stirring occasionally, until it has changed colour all over—2 to 3 minutes. Stir in the tomatoes and sherry. Bring the mixture to the boil and cook it for 2 minutes.

Spoon the kale into a hot serving dish, cover it and keep it warm. Transfer the lamb and its sauce to a second hot dish, stir in the soured cream and serve immediately, accompanied by the kale.

Stir-Fried Vegetables with Shredded Lamb

Serves 4

Working (and total) time: about 40 minutes

Calories 255, Protein 21g, Cholesterol 50mg,
Total fat 13g, Saturated fat 3g, Sodium 265mg

350 g/12 oz	*lean lamb (from the loin), cut into thin strips*
4 tbsp	*sake or dry sherry*
2 tbsp	*low-sodium soy sauce or shoyu*
1 tsp	*cornflour*
2 tbsp	*safflower oil*
1 tbsp	*finely chopped fresh ginger root*
1	*onion, peeled and sliced*
175 g/6 oz	*baby sweetcorn, halved lengthwise if large*
1	*sweet red pepper, seeded, deribbed*
175 g/6 oz	*cucumber, halved lengthwise, seeded and sliced*
175 g/6 oz	*small mange-tout, stems and strings removed*

Mix together the sake, soy sauce and cornflour in a small bowl and set the mixture aside.

Heat the oil in a wok or large, heavy sauté pan until it is hot but not smoking. Add the chopped ginger and onion slices, and stir-fry for 1 minute over high heat, then add the baby sweetcorn and continue to stir-fry for 1 more minute.

Add the strips of lamb a few at a time, stirring constantly until they are completely sealed and lightly col-

oured, then add the pepper and cucumber and stir-fry for a further minute.

Lastly, add the mange-tout and stir-fry for 1 minute. Pour the sake mixture over the meat and vegetables in the wok and bring it to the boil, stirring until the liquid thickens. Serve immediately.

Loin and Liver in Yellow Bean Sauce

Serves 4

Working time: about 20 minutes

Total time: about 30 minutes

Calories 235, Protein 22g, Cholesterol 265mg,
Total fat 13g, Saturated fat 3g, Sodium 425mg

175 g/6 oz	*lean lamb (from the loin), trimmed of fat and cut into thin strips*
175 g/6 oz	*lamb's liver, cut into thin strips*
2 tsp	*light low-sodium soy sauce*
2 tsp	*Chinese rice wine or dry sherry*
1 tsp	*sesame oil*
1½ tsp	*cornflour*
200 g/7 oz	*spring onions*
2 cm/¾ inch	*piece fresh ginger root*
1	*garlic clove*
2 tsp	*safflower oil*
½	*fresh red chilli pepper, seeded and thinly sliced*
	nori seaweed, shredded, for garnish

Yellow bean sauce

3 tbsp	*yellow bean sauce*
½ tsp	*sugar*
1 tsp	*dark low-sodium soy sauce or shoyu*
2 tsp	*Chinese rice wine or dry sherry*

Put the loin and liver strips into separate bowls. Blend together the light soy sauce, rice wine, sesame oil and cornflour and divide this marinade between the two bowls. Stir well to coat the meat thoroughly. Leave to marinate for 15 minutes. Mix together the ingredients for the yellow bean sauce and set the sauce aside.

Cut the spring onions into 6 cm (2½ inch) lengths. Cut the white sections in half lengthwise; keep the white and the green parts separate. Bruise the ginger and garlic with the side of a heavy knife.

Heat a wok over medium heat and add the safflower oil. Drop in the ginger and garlic and let them sizzle until they turn light brown. Using the tip of a spatula ub the garlic and ginger all round the wok, then re-move and discard them. Increase the heat to high. Stir-ry the loin, followed by the liver, the white parts of the spring onions and the yellow bean sauce, by con-tantly tossing and stirring each ingredient for about 5 seconds before adding the next. If the food seems about to stick and burn, lift the wok off the heat for a few seconds Add the chilli and stir-fry for another 10 seconds, then stir in the green parts of the spring on-ions.

Serve the mixture immediately, garnished with a lit-tle shredded nori.

Warm Herbed Salad

Serves 4

Working time: about 30 minutes

Total time: about 3 hours and 30 minutes
(includes marinating)

Calories 260, Protein 31g, Cholesterol 90mg,
Total fat 14g, Saturated fat 6g, Sodium 380mg

4	*lamb slices (about 125 g/4 oz each), cut from the fillet end of the leg, trimmed of fat and flattened to about 3 mm (¹/₄ inch) thick*
12.5 cl/4 fl oz	*dry white wine*
1 tbsp	*chopped fresh tarragon*
4 tsp	*chopped fresh dill*
4 tsp	*chopped fresh chervil*
1 tbsp	*safflower oil*
³/₄ tsp	*salt*
	freshly ground black pepper
100 g/3¹/₂ oz	*cucumber, cut into bâtonnets*
200 g/7 oz	*Batavian endive, washed and dried, trimmed and shredded*
2 tbsp	*crème fraîche*
3 tbsp	*thick Greek yoghurt*
¹/₄ tsp	*sugar*

Cut each slice of meat into five strips. Place the meat in a shallow dish with the wine, the tarragon and 3 teaspoons each of the dill and chervil. Leave the meat to marinate for 3 to 4 hours, turning it half way through.

Remove the meat from the marinade and dry it well on paper towels; reserve the marinade. Heat the oil in a wide, heavy frying pan until it is very hot but not smoking. Brown the meat for 30 seconds on each side, then remove it from the pan and season it with ¹/₂ teaspoon of the salt and some black pepper. Keep it warm while preparing the salad.

Skim off any fat from the pan juices, then add the cucumber bâtonnets and cook gently over medium heat until they begin to soften—about 1¹/₂ minutes. Transfer them to a large bowl and add the endive.

To make the dressing, strain the reserved marinade into the frying pan and boil it over high heat until only 3 tablespoons of liquid remain. Remove the pan from the heat, stir in the *crème fraîche* and cook over low heat for 1 minute. Again remove the pan from the heat, and stir in the yoghurt, the sugar and the remaining dill, chervil and salt. Pour the warm dressing over the endive and cucumber in the bowl, toss the salad and arrange it on four individual plates. Place the strips of lamb on top and serve immediately.

Lamb Stroganoff

Serves 4
Working (and total) time: about 25 minutes
Calories 230, Protein 29g, Cholesterol 80mg, Total fat 12g, Saturated fat 5g, Sodium 175mg

500 g/1 lb *lean lamb (from the loin), trimmed of fat
                and cut into thin strips*
1 tbsp *virgin olive oil*
1 *onion, finely chopped*
250 g/8 oz *mushrooms, thinly sliced*
4 tbsp *thick Greek yoghurt*
1 tsp *Dijon mustard*
1/4 tsp *salt*
          freshly ground black pepper
1 tbsp *chopped parsley*
1 tbsp *finely cut chives*

Heat the oil in a large, heavy frying pan over medium heat. Add the onion and cook it gently until soft but not brown—6 to 8 minutes. Transfer the onion to a plate. Add half of the lamb strips to the frying pan and cook them over high heat until they are lightly browned—1 to 2 minutes—then transfer them to the plate with the onion. Brown the remaining lamb strips, then return the first batch of lamb and the onion to the pan.

Add the mushrooms and cook over medium heat until they soften—4 to 5 minutes. Away from the heat, stir the yoghurt and mustard into the mixture, then heat it through gently for 3 to 4 minutes. Season with the salt and some black pepper.

Transfer the stroganoff to a serving dish. Sprinkle it with the parsley and chives and serve immediately.

Escalopes with Mustard and Tarragon

Serves 4

Working (and total): time about 20 minutes

Calories 255, Protein 30g, Cholesterol 75mg,
Total fat 12g, Saturated fat 5g, Sodium 140mg

4	lamb slices (about 125 g/4 oz each), from the fillet end of the leg, trimmed of fat, flattened to about 3 mm (¹/₈ inch) thick
50 g/1 oz	dry wholemeal breadcrumbs
1 tbsp	chopped fresh tarragon, or 1 tsp dried tarragon
2 tbsp	chopped parsley
¹/₂	lemon, grated rind only
	freshly ground black pepper
2 tbsp	Dijon mustard
1 tbsp	virgin olive oil
4	lemon wedges, for garnish

Mix together the breadcrumbs, tarragon, parsley, lemon rind and some pepper. Sprinkle the mixture on to a large sheet of greaseproof paper. Cut the lamb slices in half. Using a brush, lightly coat one side of each slice with the mustard. Set a slice, mustard side down, on the crumb mixture, then turn it to coat the other side. Repeat with the remaining slices.

Heat half of the oil in a large, heavy frying pan over medium-high heat and sauté four of the escalopes until they are golden-brown—1¹/₂ to 2 minutes each side. Keep them warm while you cook the remaining four escalopes in the rest of the oil. Garnish each portion with a lemon wedge and serve immediately.

Lamb and Barley Salad

Serves 4
Working time: about 20 minutes
Total time: about 2 hours (includes chilling)
Calories 265, Protein 21g, Cholesterol 50mg,
Total fat 10g, Saturated fat 4g, Sodium 275mg

350 g/12 oz	lean lamb (from the leg or loin), trimmed of fat and cut into 1 cm (*1/2 inch*) cubes
100 g/3 1/2 oz	pearl barely
1 1/2 tbsp	finely chopped fresh oregano, or 1/2 tsp dried oregano
1 1/2 tbsp	virgin olive oil
1/4 tsp	salt
	freshly ground black pepper
3 tbsp	red wine vinegar
1	large ripe tomato, seeded and chopped
1	stick celery, chopped
90 g/3 oz	red onion, chopped
	lettuce leaves, for garnish

Put the barley, half of the oregano and 3/4 litre (1 1/4 pints) of water into 2 saucepan. Bring the water to the boil, then reduce the heat to maintain a steady simmer. Cover the pan and cook the barley until it is tender—about 50 minutes. Drain the barley, transfer it to a bowl, and stir in tablespoon of the oil.

Heat the remaining oil in a heavy frying pan set over high heat. Add the lamb cubes and sprinkle them with the salt and some freshly ground pepper. Sauté the cubes, stirring frequently, until they are lightly browned—about 2 minutes. Pour in the vinegar and cook the mixture for 30 seconds longer.

Transfer the contents of the pan to the bowl with the barley. Add the tomato, celery, onion, the remaining oregano and a generous grinding of pepper. Toss the salad well and chill it for at least 1 hour.

Just before serving, arrange the lettuce leaves on a plate or platter and mound the salad on top.

Marinated Cutlets with Caper and Parsley Sauce

Serves 6

Working time: about 30 minutes
Total time: about 2 hours and 30 minutes
(includes marinating)
Calories 255, Protein 27g, Cholesterol 85mg,
Total fat 15g, Saturated fat 3g, Sodium 170mg

12	*best end of neck cutlets (about 90 g/3 oz each), trimmed of fat*
1 tsp	*virgin olive oil*
1	*garlic clove, finely chopped*
1 tbsp	*chopped parsley*
1 tsp	*chopped fresh marjoram, or $^1/_4$ tsp dried marjoram*
1 tsp	*chopped fresh thyme, or $^1/_4$ tsp dried thyme*
$^1/_4$ tsp	*salt*
$^1/_2$ tsp	*freshly ground black pepper*
	Caper and parsley sauce
1 tsp	*cornflour*
8 cl/3 fl oz	*skimmed milk*
75 g/2$^1/_2$ oz	*crème fraîche*
4	*pickled onions, finely chopped*
2 tbsp	*chopped parsley*
1 tbsp	*finely chopped capers*
	freshly ground black pepper

Using a sharp knife, scrape the ends of the rib bones free of any flesh or skin. Place the cutlets in a large shallow dish. Combine the olive oil, garlic, parsley, marjoram, thyme, salt and freshly ground pepper, and brush this mixture over both sides of the cutlets. Cover the dish and leave the cutlets to marinate in the refrigerator for 2 to 4 hours.

Preheat the grill to high while you make the sauce. Mix the cornflour with 1 tablespoon of the milk. Bring the remaining milk nearly to the boil in a small saucepan, add the cornflour paste and cook over low heat, stirring, until the milk thickens—2 to 3 minutes. Stir in the *crème fraîche*, pickled onions, parsley, capers and some pepper. Heat the sauce through, remove it from the heat and keep it warm while cooking the cutlets.

Cook the cutlets for 3 to 4 minutes on each side for rare to medium meat and serve them with the sauce.

Cutlets with Pernod

Serves 4

Working time: about 25 minutes
Total time: about 2 hours and 30 minutes
(includes marinating)
Calories 260, Protein 29g, Cholesterol 75mg, Total fat 13g, Saturated fat 6g, Sodium 280mg

8	*best end of neck cutlets (about 90 g/3 oz each), trimmed of fat*
2	*limes, finely grated rind and juice*
4 tbsp	*plain low-fat yoghurt*
2 tbsp	*Pernod or other anise-flavoured spirit*
1 tbsp	*chopped fresh thyme, or 1 tsp dried thyme*
2	*garlic cloves, crushed*
1 tsp	*muscovado sugar*
	freshly ground black pepper
1 tsp	*cornflour*
$^1/_2$ tsp	*salt*
	lime wedges, for garnish
	thyme sprigs, for garnish (optional)

Put the lime rind and juice in a shallow dish with the yoghurt, Pernod, thyme, crushed garlic, sugar and some freshly ground pepper. Whisk together with a fork, then place the lamb cutlets in the dish and turn them to coat them evenly. Cover the dish and leave the cutlets to marinate in the refrigerator for at least 2 hours, or preferably overnight.

Preheat the grill to high. Lift the cutlets out of the marinade, reserving the marinade, and grill them for 3 to 4 minutes on each side for rare to medium meat.

While the cutlets are grilling, put the cornflour into a saucepan, blend in the marinade and add the salt. Bring the sauce to the boil and simmer for 3 minutes, stirring constantly. Arrange the cutlets on a warm serving dish and garnish with the lime wedges and thyme sprigs, if you are using them. Pass the sauce separately.

Noisettes with Glazed Potatoes and Gooseberry Purée

Serves 6
Working time: about 45 minutes
Total time: about 1 hour
Calories 280, Protein 31g, Cholesterol 75mg,
Total fat 11g, Saturated fat 5g, Sodium 195mg

2	racks of lamb (about 600 g/1¹/₄ lb each), trimmed of fat, boned, tied and cut into 12 noisettes
2 tsp	virgin olive oil
	freshly ground black pepper
7 g/¹/₄ oz	unsalted butter
2	shallots, finely chopped
15 cl/¹/₄ pint	unsalted chicken stock
¹/₈ tsp	salt
400 g/14 oz	tiny new potatoes, scrubbed
	fresh chervil, for garnish

Minted gooseberry purée

500 g/1 lb	fresh gooseberries, topped and tailed, or frozen gooseberries, thawed
2	mint sprigs plus six leaves
1 tsp	light brown sugar
¹/₄ tsp	salt

Brush the noisettes with the olive oil and rub them all over with freshly ground pepper. Arrange them on a grill pan and set them aside.

To make the purée, place the gooseberries in a heavy-bottomed, non-reactive saucepan, together with the sprigs of mint, the sugar and 1 tablespoon of water. Cover and cook gently until the gooseberries are soft—15 to 30 minutes. Remove the mint sprigs and purée the gooseberries in a blender with the fresh mint leaves and the salt. Pass the purée through a nylon sieve; set it aside and keep it warm.

Melt the butter in a heavy-bottomed saucepan and gently cook the shallots, covered, until they are soft—about 5 minutes. Add the stock and salt, bring it to the boil, then add the potatoes and cook them, partly-covered, until they are tender—20 to 25 minutes. Meanwhile, preheat the grill to high.

Remove the lid from the pan and boil the stock rapidly until no liquid remains and the potatoes are glossy—about 3 minutes. Shake the pan regularly during this process to prevent the potatoes and shallots from singeing. Keep warm until ready to serve.

Grill the noisettes for 3 to 4 minutes on each side for rare to medium meat. Arrange them on a warm serving platter with the glazed potatoes and garnish with chervil. Serve the purée separately.

Crusted Butterfly Chops
with Peppercorn Sauce

Serves 4

Working time: about 40 minutes

Total time: about 1 hour

Calories 215, Protein 32g, Cholesterol 75mg,
Total fat 14g, Saturated fat 7g, Sodium 270mg

4	double loin butterfly chops (about 175 g/6 oz each), trimmed of fat, boned and secured with skewers
4	slices white bread
1	garlic clove, peeled
1	shallot, finely chopped
175 g/6 oz	button mushrooms, wiped and finely chopped
1 tsp	grated lemon rind
1 tsp	chopped fresh thyme, or 1/4 tsp dried thyme
1 tbsp	chopped parsley
1 1/2 tsp	fresh green peppercorns, or green peppercorns in brine, rinsed
15 cl/1/4 pint	unsalted chicken or veal stock
1/8 tsp	salt
2 tbsp	fresh white or brown breadcrumbs
15 g/1/2 oz	Lancashire cheese, or other white crumbly cheese, grated
2 tbsp	thick Greek yoghurt or soured cream

Preheat the oven to 180°C (350°F or Mark 4). Cut out four circles from the bread, each slightly larger in di-ameter than the butterfly chops. Bake them in the oven until they are golden-brown—20 to 25 minutes—then rub one side of each with the garlic clove and keep them warm. Preheat the grill to high.

While the croûtes are baking, brush a heavy, non-stick frying pan with oil, place it over high heat and stir-fry the chopped shallot for 2 minute. Add the mushrooms and soften them over a moderate heat for 4 minutes, then increase the heat and cook them rapidly for a minute or two to reduce excess moisture. Remove the pan from the heat, stir in the lemon rind, thyme and parsley and set the pan aside.

Grill the butterfly steaks for 4 to 6 minutes each side for rare to medium meat. Meanwhile, heat a small, shallow pan and dry-fry the peppercorns for 30 seconds. Pour in the stock and boil it rapidly until it has reduced by half—about 4 minutes. Remove the chops from the grill and set them aside. Skim the fat from the juices in the grill pan, then pour the juices into the reduced stock. Season the sauce with the salt, and set it over low heat to keep warm.

Spoon the mushroom mixture neatly on to the chops. Mix the breadcrumbs with the grated cheese, then sprinkle the breadcrumb mixture over the mushrooms. Return the chops to the grill until the cheese turns golden-brown. Remove the skewers. Set each crusted chop on top of a croûte.

Remove the sauce from the heat and stir in the yoghurt or cream. Serve the sauce with the chops.

Sweet and Spicy Grilled Lamb

Serves 4
Working time: about 1 hour
Total time: about 2 hours (includes marinating)
Calories 310, Protein 23g, Cholesterol 70mg, Total fat 8g,
Saturated fat 3g, Sodium 205mg

1 kg/2 lb *loin, boned and trimmed of fat, eye only*
freshly ground black pepper
¹/₄ tsp *ground allspice*
¹/₄ tsp *ground cloves*
2 tbsp *fresh lemon juice*

2 tbsp *light brown sugar*
Cherry ketchup
225 g/7¹/₂ oz *sweet cherries, stoned*
4 tbsp *light brown sugar*
¹/₄ tsp *salt*
6 tbsp *cider vinegar*
7.5 cm/3 inch *strip of lemon rind*
¹/₂ tsp *ground ginger*
2 *cinnamon sticks*
¹/₈ tsp *cayenne pepper*

To make the ketchup, combine the cherries, brown sugar, salt, vinegar, lemon rind, ginger, cinnamon sticks and cayenne pepper in a heavy-bottomed saucepan. Bring the mixture to a simmer and cook it until it has thickened—about 15 minutes. Discard the cinnamon sticks and pour the mixture into a food processor or blender. Purée the mixture, then strain it into a small bowl and allow it to cool.

To prepare a marinade for the meat, mix a generous grinding of pepper with the allspice, cloves, lemon juice and brown sugar in a small bowl. Put the eye of loin in a shallow dish and pour the marinade over it, rubbing the spices into the meat. Let the lamb marinate at room temperature for 1 hour, turning it every 15 minutes.

If you plan to barbecue the meat, light the charcoal about 30 minutes before cooking time, to grill, preheat the grill for about 10 minutes. Remove the lamb from the marinade and cook it for 5 to 7 minutes on each side, brushing it occasionally with any marinade remaining in the dish. Let the lamb rest for about 5 minutes before slicing it. Serve the ketchup separately.

EDITOR'S NOTE: Only the eye of the loin is used here, reserve the fillet for another recipe where lean meat is called for.

Steaks with Grated Courgettes and a Tomato Coulis

Serves 4
Working time: about 25 minutes
Total time: 45 minutes
Calories 280, Protein 31g, Cholesterol 75mg,
Total fat 13g, Saturated fat 5g, Sodium 395mg

4	boneless steaks (about 140 g/4¹/₂ oz each), cut from the fillet end of the leg and trimmed of fat, or butterfly steaks, boned
400 g/14 oz	courgettes
1 tsp	salt
1 tbsp	virgin olive oil
2 tbsp	chopped fresh marjoram, or 2 tsp dried marjoram
	freshly ground black pepper
	ribbon-thin lengthwise slices of courgette, for garnish (optional)

Tomato coulis

1 tsp	virgin olive oil
2	garlic cloves, finely chopped
750 g/1¹/₂ lb	ripe tomatoes, skinned, seeded and finely chopped, or 400 g (14 oz) canned tomatoes, chopped
1 tbsp	chopped fresh oregano, or 1 tsp dried oregano
1 tsp	chopped fresh marjoram, or ¹/₄ tsp dried marjoram
	freshly ground black pepper
8 cl/3 fl oz	medium-dry white wine

Trim the courgettes and grate them coarsely, the transfer them to a sieve set over a bowl. Stir in half a teaspoon of the salt and allow the courgettes to stand for 30 minutes.

Meanwhile, brush the steaks with the oil, rub them with half of the marjoram and sprinkle them with black pepper. Using cocktail sticks or skewers, pin the steaks into neat rounds and set them aside.

To make the tomato coulis, heat the oil in a heavy-bottomed saucepan. Add the garlic and cook it for minute over medium-high heat. Add the tomatoes, oregano, marjoram and some pepper. Cook until the tomatoes are reduced to a purée—about 10 minutes. Add the wine, heat the coulis through and keep warm. Preheat the grill to medium.

Season the steaks with the remaining salt and grill them for 5 to 6 minutes each side for rare to medium meat. While they are grilling, squeeze the courgette dry with your hands and stir-fry them with the remaining marjoram in a non-stick saucepan over medium low heat until they soften—about 3 minutes.

When the steaks are cooked, remove the cocktail sticks or skewers. Spread the courgette mixture evenly on top of each steak. Pour a little of the tomato coulis on to each of four warmed plates, and arrange the steaks on top. Garnish with the strips of courgette if you are using them, and serve immediately.

Grilled Lamb with Chutney Glaze and Mint

Serves 10
Working time: about 30 minutes
Total time: about 1 hour and 15 minutes
Calories 200, Protein 23g, Cholesterol 75mg, Total fat 8g,
Saturated fat 3g, Sodium 135mg

2.5 kg/5 lb	*leg of lamb, trimmed of fat and boned*
1 tbsp	*safflower oil*
1/4 tsp	*salt*
	freshly ground black pepper
4 tbsp	*chopped mint*
	mint sprigs, for garnish

Chutney glaze

1/4 litre/8 fl oz	*unsalted brown or chicken stock*
4 tbsp	*mango chutney*
1/2 tbsp	*dry mustard*
1 tbsp	*cider vinegar*
1/2 tbsp	*cornflour, mixed with 1 tbsp water*

First, prepare the lamb. Spread the boned leg of lamb flat on a work surface with the cut side of the meat facing upwards. Cut out the membranes and tendons and discard them. Starting from the centre of the meat slice horizontally into the flesh at one side of the leg making sure that you do not cut completely through the meat. Open out the resulting flap, then slice into the opposite side of the leg and open it out in a similar manner. The meat should be no more than 5 cm (2 inches) thick.

If you plan to barbecue the lamb, light the charcoal about 30 minutes before cooking time; to grill the meat, preheat the grill for 10 minutes.

To make the chutney glaze, combine the stock and the mango chutney in a small saucepan and bring the mixture to a simmer over medium heat. Stir the mustard and the cider vinegar into the cornflour paste and then whisk this mixture into the simmering stock and chutney. Cook the glaze, stirring continuously, until it thickens—about 1 minute. Remove the pan from the heat and set the glaze aside.

With your fingers, rub both sides of the lamb with the safflower oil. Grill the lamb, turning it every 5 minutes, until it is well browned on both sides—about 20 minutes in all. Sprinkle the salt and some freshly ground black pepper on the lamb and brush it with some of the chutney glaze. Continue cooking the lamb, turning and basting it frequently with the glaze for about another 10 minutes. Pour the remaining chutney glaze into a small serving bowl.

Transfer the lamb to a cutting board and sprinkle it with the chopped mint. Allow the meat to stand for 1 minutes before carving it into slices. Arrange the slices of lamb on a warm serving platter and serve accompanied by the remaining chutney glaze and garnished with mint sprigs.

Leg of Lamb in Spiced Apple Sauce

Serves 12

Working time: about 45 minutes

Total time: about 2 hours and 25 minutes
(includes marinating)

Calories 225, Protein 30g, Cholesterol 80mg, Total fat 9g,
Saturated fat 4g, Sodium 135mg

2.5 kg/5 lb	leg of lamb, trimmed of fat and boned
4 tbsp	cider vinegar
1	onion, finely chopped
2	garlic cloves, finely chopped
1 tbsp	finely chopped fresh sage, or 1½ tsp dried sage
½ tsp	salt
1 tbsp	freshly ground black pepper
1 tbsp	safflower oil

Spiced apple sauce

300 g/10 oz	cooking apples, peeled, cored and sliced
30 g/1 oz	sugar
2	cloves
¼ tsp	ground cinnamon
⅛ tsp	ground allspice

To make the apple sauce, cook the apples gently in a heavy-bottomed saucepan with 1 tablespoon of water, until they are soft and fluffy. Drain off any excess liquid then purée the apples by pressing them through a nylon sieve. Return the purée to the saucepan, add the sugar, cloves, ground cinnamon and allspice, and cook the sauce over low heat, stirring occasionally, until the mixture has reduced to about 12.5 cl (4 fl oz) and has a thick spreading consistency. Remove the cloves and set the sauce aside to cool a little while you prepare the meat.

Spread the boned leg of lamb flat on a work surface with the cut side of the meat facing upwards. Cut out the membranes and tendons and discard them. Starting from the centre of the meat, slice horizontally into the flesh at one side of the leg, making sure that you do not cut completely through the meat. Open out the resulting flap, then slice into the opposite side of the leg and open it out in a similar manner. The meat should be no more than 5 cm (2 inches) thick.

Put the apple sauce into a large bowl and mix in the vinegar, onion, garlic, sage, salt, pepper and oil. Put the butterflied lamb into the bowl and spread the apple sauce mixture thickly all over it. Leave the lamb in the bowl to marinate at room temperature for about 1 hour, turning it after 30 minutes.

If you plan to barbecue the lamb, light the charcoal about 30 minutes before cooking time; to grill it preheat the grill for 10 minutes. Remove the lamb from the marinade, holding it over the bowl to allow any excess marinade to drip off. Reserve the marinade.

Cook the lamb for 12 minutes on each side for medium-rare meat. Baste the lamb from time to time with the reserved marinade.

Leave the lamb to rest for about 15 minutes, then carve it into slices and serve.

Flambéed Kebabs

Serves 6

Working time: about 50 minutes

Total time: about 3 hours and 50 minutes

(includes marinating)

Calories 255, Protein 30g, Cholesterol 75mg,

Total fat 11g, Saturated fat 4g, Sodium 100mg

750 g/1¹/₂ lb	*eye and fillet of loin, trimmed of fat and cut into 24 cubes*
1	*large courgette, thickly sliced*
¹/₂	*sweet green pepper, seeded and cut into 6 by 2.5 cm (2¹/₂ by 1 inch) strips*
¹/₂	*sweet red pepper, seeded and cut into 6 by 2.5 cm (2¹/₂ by 1 inch) strips*
1	*large onion, cut into 12 wedges*
2	*oranges, rind and pith removed, halved and cut into 1 cm (¹/₂ inch) slices*
1	*firm ripe mango, peeled and cut into six pieces*
1 tbsp	*virgin olive oil*
4 tbsp	*brandy*

Orange and honey marinade

1	*orange, finely grated rind and strained juice only*
3 tbsp	*clear honey*
1	*onion, finely grated*
4	*garlic cloves, crushed*
1 tbsp	*tomato paste*
1 tbsp	*virgin olive oil*
1 tbsp	*paprika*
¹/₂ tsp	*salt*
¹/₄ tsp	*cayenne pepper*

Put all of the marinade ingredients into a large mixing bowl and stir them well together. Add the cubes of lamb and stir until they are thoroughly coated with the marinade. Cover the bowl and allow the lamb to marinate at room temperature for 3 to 4 hours, turning it from time to time

When you are ready to assemble the kebabs, blanch the courgette and peppers in boiling water for 2 to 3 minutes to soften them slightly. Transfer the vegetables to a colander and refresh them under cold running water. Drain well.

Preheat the grill to its highest setting. Thread the marinated lamb and pieces of courgette, pepper, onion, orange and mango alternately on six kebab skewers. Place the skewers on the grill rack and sprinkle them with the olive oil. Grill the kebabs for 10 to 15 minutes, carefully turning the skewers three or four times to ensure that they cook evenly. At the end of this time the lamb should be cooked, yet still slightly pink in the centre.

When the kebabs are ready, place them on a warmed dish. Put the brandy into a small shallow sauté pan and warm it over low heat for about 10 seconds. Standing well back, ignite the brandy in the pan with a taper and pour it, flaming, over the kebabs. Arrange the kebabs on a serving platter.

Lamb Tikka

Working time: about 30 minutes
Total time: about 5 hours (includes marinating)
Calories 255, Protein 32g, Cholesterol 75mg, Total fat 9g,
Saturated fat 4g, Sodium 100mg

500 g/1 lb	lean lamb (from the loin or fillet end of leg), trimmed of fat and cut into 4 cm (1¹/₂ inch) cubes
2. 5 cm/1 inch	piece fresh ginger root, peeled and coarsely chopped
2	garlic cloves, coarsely chopped
2	green chilli peppers, seeded and coarsely chopped
2 tsp	cumin seeds
1 tsp	ground turmeric
¹/₂ tsp	ground fenugreek
12	mint leaves
15 cl/¹/₄ pint	plain low-fat yoghurt
1 tbsp	fresh lime juice
2	star anise pods
350 g/12 oz	fresh pineapple, cut into chunks

Put the meat in a bowl. In a blender or food processor, purée the ginger, garlic, chillies, cumin, turmeric, fenugreek and mint leaves. Add the yoghurt and lime juice and blend to mix. Pour the purée over the meat, add the star anise and mix well to coat the meat thoroughly. Leave the lamb to marinate in a cool place for 4 to 6 hours, stirring occasionally.

Preheat the grill to hot. Thread the cubes of meat and pineapple alternately on to four metal kebab skewers; reserve the marinade. Place the kebabs on a grill rack and grill until the lamb is cooked but still slightly pink in the centre—10 to 15 minutes. Turn the skewers frequently and baste the meat with the reserved marinade while grilling.

Kebabs with Olive-Mint Sauce

Serves 4

Working time: about 25 minutes
Total time: about 40 minutes
Calories 240, Protein 24g, Cholesterol 75mg,
Total fat 12g, Saturated fat 3g, Sodium 295mg

600 g/1 1/4 lb	*lean lamb (from the loin or fillet end of leg), trimmed of fat and cut into 16 cubes*
30g/1 oz	*mint, chopped*
6	*oil-cured black olives, stoned and finely chopped*
1 tbsp	*virgin olive oil*
1/2 tsp	*ground allspice*
	freshly ground black pepper
2	*onions, each cut into six wedges*
1/2	*sweet green pepper, seeded, deribbed and cut into eight pieces*
1/2	*red apple, cored and cut into eight pieces*
1/4 litre/8 fl oz	*unsalted brown or chicken stock*

If you plan to barbecue the lamb, light the charcoal about 30 minutes before cooking time; to grill, preheat the grill for 10 minutes.

Put the lamb cubes into a bowl with 3 tablespoons of the mint, half of the olives, 1/2 tablespoon of the oil, 1/4 teaspoon of the allspice and a generous grinding of pepper. Stir the lamb cubes to coat them evenly with the marinade, then set the bowl aside at room temperature while you prepare the other ingredients.

Gently toss together the onions, green pepper, apple, 3 tablespoons of the remaining mint, the remaining olive oil and allspice and some black pepper in another bowl, and set it aside.

Pour the stock into a small saucepan over medium heat, then stir in the remaining olives, the remaining mint and the salt. Cook the sauce until only about 6 tablespoons remain—about 10 minutes. Remove the pan from the heat and set it aside.

Thread the lamb cubes and the vegetable and apple chunks on to four skewers. Grill the kebabs for 3 to 4 minutes on each side for medium meat. Transfer them to a platter. Reheat the sauce, pour it over the kebabs and serve immediately.

Lamb Sausages on Skewers

Serves 4

Working time: about 30 minutes

Total time: about 1 hour and 10 minutes

Calories 245, Protein 26g, Cholesterol 75mg,
Total fat 11g, Saturated fat 4g, Sodium 320mg

600 g/1¼ lb	lean lamb (from the leg or loin), trimmed of fat and minced
1	large ripe tomato, seeded and chopped
¼ tsp	salt
	freshly ground black pepper
1 tsp	sugar
1 tbsp	red wine vinegar
3 tbsp	chopped parsley
1 tbsp	chopped fresh oregano, or 1 tsp dried oregano
1 tbsp	virgin olive oil
30 g/1 oz	dry breadcrumbs
2	spring onions, trimmed and thinly sliced
½ tsp	capers, rinsed
2.5 cl/4 fl oz	plain low-fat yoghurt

Put the tomato, half of the salt, some pepper, the sugar and the vinegar into a heavy frying pan set over medium heat. Cook the mixture, stirring frequently, until only about 4 tablespoons remain—about 20 minutes. Transfer the mixture to a bowl and let it cool to room temperature.

In a large bowl, combine the minced lamb with 2 tablespoons of the parsley, the oregano, egg white, half of the oil, the breadcrumbs, half of the spring onions, the remaining salt and some pepper. Stir the cooled tomato mixture into the lamb mixture and refrigerate the bowl until the contents are thoroughly chilled—about 30 minutes.

If you plan to barbecue the sausages, light the charcoal about 30 minutes before cooking time; to grill, preheat the grill for 10 minutes.

Divide the lamb mixture into four portions and form each one into a sausage shape about 10 cm (4 inches) long. Thread each sausage on to a skewer, keeping the meat pressed firmly in place.

Pour the remaining oil on to a large, flat plate. Lightly coat the sausages by rolling them in the oil. Grill or barbecue the sausages, turning the skewers every now and then, until the meat is lightly browned—8 to 10 minutes.

Meanwhile, finely chop the remaining parsley with the remaining spring onions and the capers. Transfer the chopped parsley mixture to a small bowl and whisk in the yoghurt and some pepper. Serve the sausages immediately, passing the sauce separately.

Kofta with Onion Sauce

Serves 4
Working time: about 30 minutes
Total time: about 40 minutes
Calories 260, Protein 27g, Cholesterol 80mg,
Total fat 14g, Saturated fat 5g, Sodium 195mg

500 g/1 lb	*lean lamb (from the leg or loin), trimmed of fat and minced*
1	*onion, finely chopped*
60 g/2 oz	*pitted olives, finely chopped*
2 tbsp	*chopped fresh coriander*
1 tbsp	*Worcester sauce*
¼ tsp	*salt*
	freshly ground black pepper
30 g/1 oz	*caul (optional)*

Onion sauce

15 g/¹/₂ oz	*polyunsaturated margarine*
1	*red onion, finely chopped*
1 tsp	*cumin seeds*
2 tbsp	*raspberry or cider vinegar*
1 tbsp	*cornflour*
30 cl/¹/₂ pint	*unsalted brown stock*
¹/₈ tsp	*salt*
	freshly ground black pepper

First, make the onion sauce. Melt the margarine in a sauté pan or heavy frying pan. Add the onion and cumin seeds, and cook them over medium heat until the onions are soft—about 4 minutes. Add the vinegar and continue cooking until the liquid reduces to a thick syrup. Mix the cornflour to a paste with 2 tablespoons of the stock. Add the remaining stock to the pan and bring it to the boil. Add the cornflour paste and stir until the sauce thickens—2 to 3 minutes. Season the sauce with the salt and some black pepper; keep warm while you prepare the kofta.

Combine the lamb, onion, olives, coriander, Worcester sauce, salt and some pepper in a bowl and mix thoroughly by hand. Shape the meat into 20 thick sausages, each about 4 cm (1¹/₂ inches) long. If you like, wrap eight of the sausages with pieces of caul. Carefully thread the sausages on to four long metal skewers, alternating caul-wrapped ones with plain.

Preheat the grill to high and cook the kofta for 10 minutes, turning them once. Serve the kofta hot with the onion sauce.

EDITOR'S NOTE: Caul, the weblike fatty membrane that surrounds a pigs stomach, gives the meat a distinctive flavour and helps moisten lean minced meat during grilling.

Lamb and Mushroom Burgers

Serves 4
Working time: about 30 minutes
Total time: about 1 hour and 5 minutes
Calories 350, Protein 36g, Cholesterol 80mg,
Total fat 10g, Saturated fat 5g, Sodium 450mg

500 g/1 lb	lean lamb (from the leg or loin), trimmed of fat and minced
3 tbsp	fresh granary or wholemeal breadcrumbs
2 tbsp	fresh orange juice
1/4 tsp	finely grated lemon rind
1 tbsp	chopped parsley
2 tsp	finely cut chives
1/8 tsp	dried marjoram
1/8 tsp	salt
	freshly ground black pepper
125 g/4 oz	button mushrooms, wiped and finely chopped
4	granary baps, split in half
	carrot ribbons, for garnish
	finely chopped celery, for garnish
	shredded cabbage, for garnish
	flat-leaf parsley, for garnish

Mustard sauce

1 tbsp	grainy mustard
4 tbsp	fromage frais
1 tbsp	finely cut chives
	freshly ground black pepper

Put the lamb, breadcrumbs, orange juice, lemon rind, parsley, chives, marjoram, salt and some pepper in a bowl and mix them thoroughly by hand. Set the bowl aside. Heat a heavy non-stick frying pan, brush it with oil, add the mushrooms and sauté them over high heat for 3 minutes, stirring them constantly. Allow the mushrooms to cool, then add them to the meat mixture. Shape the mixture into four burgers, each about 10 cm (4 inches) in diameter. Cover and refrigerate them for 30 minutes.

Meanwhile, combine the ingredients for the mustard sauce in a mixing bowl. Set the sauce aside.

Preheat the grill to hot, and cook the burgers for about 4 minutes on each side for medium meat. Toast the baps on the cut sides. Place each burger on the bottom half of a bap, garnish with the carrot, celery, cabbage and parsley, spoon on a portion of the mustard sauce and top with the other half of the bap.

Leg of Lamb
with Pomegranate Sauce

Serves 8

Working time: about 30 minutes

Total time: about 1 hour and 30 minutes

Calories 250, Protein 30g, Cholesterol 90mg, Total fat 8g,
Saturated fat 4g, Sodium 130mg

2.25 kg/4½ lb	*leg of lamb, trimmed of fat*
1 tbsp	*fresh thyme*
1	*pomegranate*
1	*lime, finely grated rind and juice only*
1½ tbsp	*redcurrant jelly*
	finely grated lime rind, for garnish
	watercress, for garnish

Pomegranate sauce

3	*pomegranates*
4 tbsp	*redcurrant jelly*
1 tbsp	*caster sugar*
2	*limes, julienned rind and juice only*
1½ tbsp	*cornflour*
8 cl/3 fl oz	*rose wine*

Preheat the oven to 200°C (400°F or Mark 6).

Make four or five incisions into the flesh of the lamb and fill them with the thyme. Place the leg of lamb in a roasting pan.

Cut open the pomegranate and scoop out the seeds. Reserve one third of the seeds for garnish. Using a wooden spoon, press all the juice from the remaining seeds through a nylon sieve into a bowl. Stir the lime rind and juice into the pomegranate juice, then pour half of the combined juices over the lamb, coating the entire surface of the meat.

Place the joint in the oven and roast it, basting frequently, for 1 to 1¼ hours for rare to medium meat. Half way through the cooking time, pour the remaining lime and pomegranate juices over the lamb.

Remove the lamb from the oven, transfer it to a warm platter and allow it to rest in a warm place for about 20 minutes.

Meanwhile, make the pomegranate sauce. Cut open the pomegranates and scoop out the seeds into a nylon sieve set over a non-reactive saucepan. Press the juice from the seeds through the sieve. Stir in the redcurrant jelly, sugar and lime juice, then heat the mixture gently until the jelly and sugar have dissolved. Cook gently for 10 minutes. Blend the cornflour with the rose wine and stir it into the sauce. Bring it to the boil and continue to cook, stirring, until the mixture thickens and clears—2 to 3 minutes. Add the julienned lime rind, reduce the heat and simmer for a further 5 minutes, stirring frequently. Transfer the sauce to a warmed sauceboat.

Just before you are ready to carve, bring the redcurrant jelly to the boil and brush it over the meat. Sprinkle the meat with the reserved pomegranate seeds; garnish with the finely grated lime rind and watercress. Serve the sauce separately.

Roast Leg with Herbs and Garlic

Serves 8
Working time: about 30 minutes
Total time: about 3 hours (includes marinating)
Calories 260, Protein 8g, Cholesterol 100mg,
Total fat 12g, Saturated fat 5g, Sodium 195mg

2.5 kg/5 lb	*leg of lamb, trimmed of fat*
3	*garlic cloves*
1 tsp	*salt*
2 tbsp	*chopped mixed fresh herbs (thyme, sage, rosemary, oregano), or 2 tsp mixed dried herbs*
1 tbsp	*finely chopped parsley*
1 tbsp	*virgin olive oil*

Using a small pointed knife, make 10 to 12 deep, evenly spaced incisions into the flesh of the lamb.

With a pestle and mortar, crush together the garlic cloves and salt to make a creamy paste. Add the mixed herbs and the parsley. Using your fingers or a small teaspoon, fill each incision in the lamb with the herb and garlic paste. Rub the olive oil all over the leg, then place it in a roasting pan and set it aside in a cool place to marinate for 1 hour. Preheat the oven to 220°C (425°F or Mark 7).

Roast the leg for 15 minutes, then reduce the oven temperature to 190°C (375°F or Mark 5) and continue roasting for 50 minutes to 1 hour for rare to medium meat, basting the leg frequently with the pan juices. Transfer the leg to a serving dish, cover it loosely with foil and allow it to rest in a warm place for 20 to 30 minutes before carving.

Leg of Lamb with Pear Mustard

Serves 10

Working time: about 1 hour

Total time: about 2 hours and 15 minutes

Calories 225, Protein 24g, Cholesterol 75mg, Total fat 9g,
Saturated fat 3g, Sodium 430mg

2.5 kg/5 lb	leg of lamb, trimmed of fat, the pelvic and thigh bones removed, the shank bone left in place
1/2 tbsp	Dijon mustard
1 tbsp	safflower oil
1/4 tsp	salt
3	bunches spring onions trimmed and cut into 2.5 cm (1 inch) lengths

Pear mustard

1/2 tbsp	safflower oil
750 g/1 1/2 lb	pears, peeled, cored and coarsely chopped
1/4 litre/8 fl oz	unsalted brown or chicken stock
1 1/2 tbsp	fresh lemon juice
1	shallot, finely chopped, or 1 spring onion, white part only, finely chopped
1	garlic clove, finely chopped
1 1/4 tsp	salt
	freshly ground black pepper
1 1/2 tbsp	Dijon mustard

To make the pear mustard, heat the oil in a heavy bottomed saucepan set over medium-high heat. Add the pears and cook them, stirring frequently, until the juice is syrupy and lightly browned—15 to 20 minutes. Add the stock, lemon juice, shallot or spring onion, garlic, salt, some pepper and the mustard. Reduce the heat to medium and simmer the mixture, stirring occasionally, until only about 35 cl (12 fl oz) remain—15 to 20 minutes. Transfer the pear mustard to a food processor or a blender and purée it until smooth.

Meanwhile, preheat the oven to 180°C (350°F or Mark 4) and prepare the leg of lamb for roasting. Rub the Dijon mustard over the exposed inner surface of the leg. Fold the meat over to enclose the mustard, then tie the leg securely with string. Heat the oil in a large, shallow fireproof casserole set over high heat. When the oil is hot, add the leg of lamb and brown it evenly on all sides—about 10 minutes. Sprinkle the lamb with the salt and transfer the casserole to the oven. Roast the lamb for 20 minutes.

Remove the lamb from the oven and coat it with about one third of the pear mustard, then roast it for 40 minutes more. Brush the lamb with about half of the remaining pear mustard. Increase the oven temperature to 240°C (475°F or Mark 9) and cook the lamb until the pear mustard is lightly browned in places—10 to 15 minutes. Remove from the oven and let it rest in a warm place for 20 minutes.

Blanch the spring onion pieces in boiling water for 1 minute, then drain them and divide them among 10 warmed dinner plates. Slice the lamb and arrange the slices on the spring onions; spoon a little of the remaining pear mustard on top before serving.

Leg Roasted with Ginger

Serves 10
Working time: about 25 minutes
Total time: about 4 hours and 40 minutes
(includes marinating)
Calories 185, Protein 24g, Cholesterol 75g, Total fat 7g,
Saturated fat 3g, Sodium 170mg

2.5 kg/5 lb	leg of lamb, trimmed of fat
3 tbsp	finely chopped fresh ginger root
3	garlic cloves, finely chopped
2 tsp	low-sodium soy sauce or shoyu
1/4 tsp	dark sesame oil
1 tsp	rice vinegar or distilled white vinegar
6 tbsp	mirin or sweet sherry
1/8 tsp	white pepper

Soy and sesame sauce

1 tbsp	low-sodium soy sauce or shoyu
2 tbsp	mirin or sweet sherry
1 tsp	sesame seeds
2 tsp	rice vinegar or distilled white vinegar
1	spring onion, trimmed and thinly sliced
1	small carrot, sliced into thin rounds
2 tbsp	chopped fresh ginger root
12.5 cl/4 fl oz	unsalted brown or chicken stock

With a knife, lightly score the surface of the lamb in a crisscross pattern. Transfer the lamb to a shallow baking dish. Mix the ginger, garlic, soy sauce, sesame oil, vinegar, mirin or sherry and pepper in a small bowl. Pour this marinade over the lamb and refrigerate it for at least 3 hours, or as long as overnight. From time to time, baste the lamb with the marinade.

Towards the end of the marinating time, preheat the oven to 230°C (450°F or Mark 8). Transfer the lamb to a roasting pan, reserving the marinade, and roast for 10 minutes. Reduce the oven temperature to 180°C (350°F or Mark 4) and continue roasting the lamb for 1 hour for medium-rare meat. Baste the lamb from time to time with the reserved marinade during this period. Let the lamb rest in a warm place for 20 minutes before carving it.

While the lamb is resting, combine the sauce ingredients. Serve the sauce at room temperature with the sliced lamb.

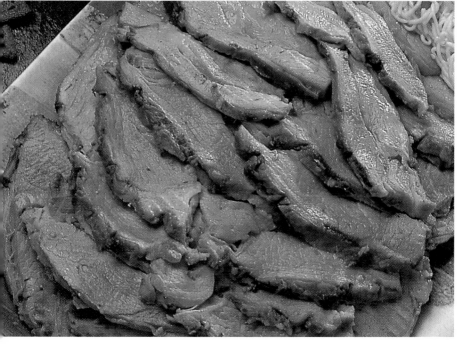

Garlic-Studded Lamb Shanks with Roasted Onions

Serves 4

Working time: about 20 minutes

Total time: about 2 hours

Calories 285, Protein 31g, Cholesterol 85mg, Total fat 9g, Saturated fat 3g, Sodium 290mg

4	lamb shanks (about 350 g/12 oz each), trimmed
6	garlic cloves, each cut lengthwise into four slices
1/2 tbsp	virgin olive oil
1 tbsp	finely chopped fresh rosemary, or 1/2 tbsp dried rosemary
	freshly ground black pepper
1/4 tsp	salt
4	onions, unpeeled
6	carrots, cut into bâtonnets and blanched for 1 minute in boiling water

Preheat the oven to 180°C (350°F or Mark 4).

With the point of a knife, make an incision in the flesh of a shank, press a garlic slice deep into the opening. Repeat the process to insert six garlic slices into each shank. Rub the shanks with the oil, then sprinkle them with the rosemary and pepper. Put the shanks in a heavy roasting pan and roast them until they are very tender—1 1/2 to 2 hours.

After the lamb shanks have been roasting for 45 minutes, sprinkle them with the salt. Wrap the onions individually in aluminium foil and set them in the oven next to the roasting pan.

When the shanks are done, transfer them to a serving platter. Skim off the fat that has collected in the roasting pan, leaving any caramelized juices in the pan. Set the pan on the stove top over medium heat. Add the blanched carrots and cook them, stirring occasionally, for 2 minutes. Pour 4 tablespoons of water into the pan and bring the liquid to a simmer, scraping up the caramelized pan juices with a wooden spoon.

Transfer the carrots and the sauce to the platter. Unwrap the onions, cut off 1 cm (1/2 inch) from their tops and set them on the platter just before serving.

EDITOR'S NOTE: Shanks, the knuckle end of the hind leg or fore leg, are not always available and may have to be ordered from the butcher in advance. If unobtainable, use chump chops (about 175 g/6 oz each). Prepare them in the same way as the shanks, but cut the cooking time by half.

Leg of Lamb Stuffed with Vegetables

Serves 10

Working time: about 40 minutes

Total time: about 2 hours

Calories 240, Protein 25g, Cholesterol 75mg,
Total fat 11g, Saturated fat 4g, Sodium 235mg

2.5 kg/5 lb	leg of lamb, trimmed of fat and boned
2 tbsp	safflower oil
1	large carrot, julienned
1	large courgette, julienned
1	large yellow squash, julienned
2.5 cl/4 fl oz	dry sherry
30 g/1 oz	Parmesan cheese, freshly grated
½ tsp	salt
	freshly ground black pepper
1 tbsp	fresh thyme, or 2 tsp dried thyme
litre/8 fl oz	unsalted brown or chicken stock
2 tbsp	finely chopped shallot or onion
1½ tbsp	cornflour, mixed with 2 tbsp water

prepare the stuffing, heat 1 tablespoon of the oil in
arge, shallow fireproof casserole over medium heat.
dd the carrot and sauté it, stirring often, for 2 min-
es. Stir in the courgette and squash, and cook the
getables until the carrot is barely tender— about 2
nutes more. Remove the casserole from the heat
d pour in 2 tablespoons of the sherry. Add the
rmesan cheese and toss the stuffing to mix it well.

Preheat the oven to 170°C (325°F or Mark 3). Spread
out the boned leg of lamb on a work surface and season it with half the salt, some pepper and half the
thyme. Spread the stuffing over the leg of lamb and
roll it up as you would a Swiss roll. Tie the leg of lamb
with string to secure it.

Wipe out the casserole and heat the remaining oil in
it over high heat. Add the lamb roll and brown it on all
sides—2 to 3 minutes altogether. Put the casserole
into the oven and roast the lamb until it is tender—
about 1 hour. Transfer the roast to a serving platter
and set it aside to rest in a warm place.

Skim off the fat and set the casserole on the stove
top over low heat. Add the stock, the remaining thyme,
the shallot or onion and the remaining sherry to the
casserole, then scrape the bottom with a wooden
spoon to dissolve the caramelized roasting juices. Increase the heat to medium-high and boil the liquid until
about one third of it remains—7 to 10 minutes. Reduce the heat to low and whisk in the cornflour mixture. Cook the sauce, stirring continuously, until it has
thickened—about 1 minute. Season the sauce with
the remaining salt and some pepper

Cut the roast into slices. Pour the sauce into a
warmed sauceboat and serve it separately.

Roast Shoulder with Rosemary

Serves 12
Working time: about 40 minutes
Total time: about 3 hours (includes marinating)
Calories 310, Protein 20g, Cholesterol 75mg,
Total fat 12g, Saturated fat 5g, Sodium 130mg

2.5 kg/3 lb	*shoulder of lamb, trimmed of fat*
1 tbsp	*virgin olive oil*
2 tsp	*mixed dried herbs*
1/2 tsp	*salt*
4	*long rosemary sprigs*
1 1/2 tsp	*plain flour*
60 cl/1 pint	*unsalted chicken or brown stock*
	freshly ground black pepper

Make four diagonal incisions with a sharp knife across the shoulder, almost down to the bone. Rub the olive oil, mixed herbs and salt all over the lamb, then insert the rosemary sprigs in the diagonal cuts. Place the shoulder in a roasting pan and set it aside in a cool place to marinate for 1 hour. Preheat the oven to 220°C (425°F or Mark 7).

Roast the shoulder for 15 minutes, then reduce the oven temperature to 190°C (375°F or Mark 5) and roast the meat for a further 45 minutes to 1 hour for rare to medium meat, basting frequently with the pan juices. Transfer the shoulder to a serving dish, cover it loosely with foil and set it aside to rest in a warm place while you make the gravy.

Tip the roasting pan slightly so that the juices run to one corner, then skim off any fat. Sprinkle the flour over the juices left in the pan and stir well with a wooden spoon until the juices and flour are smoothly blended. Gradually add the stock, stirring continuously. Place the pan over moderate heat and bring the gravy to the boil, stirring all the time until it thickens; season with some black pepper. Reduce the heat to low and simmer for 6 to 8 minutes, stirring occasionally. Strain the gravy through a sieve into a warmed gravy boat and serve it with the roast shoulder.

Shoulder Stuffed with Wild Rice and Spinach

Serves 12

Working time: about 1 hour

Total time: about 4 hours

Calories 225, Protein 22g, Cholesterol 75mg,
Total fat 13g, Saturated fat 5g, Sodium 140mg

1.5 kg/3 lb	shoulder of lamb, boned and trimmed of fat
60 g/2 oz	wild rice
2 tsp	virgin olive oil
4	shallots, coarsely chopped
175 g/6 oz	celeriac, grated
175 g/6 oz	fresh spinach, washed, stems removed
1/2 tsp	finely grated nutmeg
3/4 tsp	salt
	freshly ground black pepper
0 cl/1/2 pint	unsalted chicken stock
1 tsp	cornflour

make the stuffing, wash the wild rice and put it into
arge saucepan in twice its volume of water. Bring
e water to the boil, cover the pan and simmer until
e husks have split and the rice is soft—50 minutes
1 hour. Drain the rice and allow it to cool. Heat the
in a frying pan, add the shallots and cook them over
ry low heat until they are soft but not brown. Add

the celeriac and continue cooking until it begins to look
transparent—about 3 minutes—then add the spinach
and cook for about 1 minute, until it wilts. Blend this
mixture very briefly in a food processor to make a
rough-textured purée; do not over process. Mix the
purée with the wild rice, and season with the nutmeg,
1/2 teaspoon of the salt and some black pepper.

Preheat the oven to 230°C (450°F or Mark 8). Stuff
and tie the shoulder into a melon shape. Put the lamb
in a roasting pan and season the outside with the remaining salt and some pepper. Roast the lamb in the
oven until it is well browned—10 to 15 minutes—then
reduce the oven temperature to 200°C (400°F or Mark
6) and cook for a further 1 1/4 to 1 1/2 hours for medium-
rare to medium meat. Transfer the lamb to a carving
board and allow it to rest in a warm place for 15 minutes.

While the meat is resting, make the gravy. Skim off
any fat from the surface of the roasting juices and transfer the pan to the stove top. Add the stock and boil it
over high heat, stirring to loosen any sediment from
the bottom of the pan. Mix the cornflour with 1 tablespoon of water and add it to the pan, stirring constantly
until the gravy thickens—2 to 3 minutes. Season with
black pepper. Cut off the string and carve the lamb
into wedges. Serve the gravy separately.

Roast Saddle of Lamb with Plum Sauce

Serves 12

Working time: about 1 hour

Total time: about 2 hours and 40 minutes

Calories 335, Protein 28g, Cholesterol 75mg,
Total fat 14g, Saturated fat 6g, Sodium 180mg

4.5 kg/10 lb	*saddle of lamb*
1 tbsp	*virgin olive oil*
2 tbsp	*demerara sugar*
³/₄ tsp	*salt*
	freshly ground black pepper
750 g/1¹/₂ lb	*large purple plums, halved and stoned*
60 cl/1 pint	*red wine*
2.5 cm/1 inch	*piece cinnamon stick*
15 cl/¹/₄ pint	*unsalted chicken stock*

Fruit garnish

3	*dessert apples*
60 g/2 oz	*caster sugar*
2 tbsp	*fresh lemon juice*
6	*large purple plums, halved, stoned and sliced*

Preheat the oven to 220°C (425°F or Mark 7). Spread the saddle of lamb out flat on a cutting board and trim off the fatty strip, or apron, of flesh along each side; leave just enough to overlap slightly when tucked underneath the saddle. Carefully remove excess fat from the meat.

Rub the olive oil all over the meat, then sprinkle it with the sugar, ¹/₂ teaspoon of the salt and some black pepper. Tuck the side flaps neatly under the saddle and place it in a large roasting pan.

Roast the saddle for 20 minutes, then reduce the oven temperature to 180°C (350°F or Mark 4) and place the halved plums in the roasting pan, tucking them

closely round the lamb. Pour half of the wine over the lamb and add the piece of cinnamon. Continue roasting for 1¹/₄ to 1¹/₂ hours for rare to medium meat. Baste the meat frequently while it roasts; each time you baste, add some more of the wine until it is all used up.

Ten minutes before the lamb is cooked, begin to prepare the garnish. Peel and core the apples and cut them into 5 mm (¹/₄ inch) thick rings. Put the caster sugar into a wide, shallow, non-reactive saucepan with the lemon juice and 15 cl (¹/₄ pint) of cold water. Heat gently until the sugar dissolves. Cook the apple rings in the sugar syrup until they are soft but still firm—3 to 5 minutes. Using a slotted spoon, transfer the apple rings to a plate. Cover the apples and keep them warm. Add the sliced plums to the syrup in the pan and cook them until they begin to soften—about 1 minute. Transfer the plums to the plate with the apple rings. Reduce the syrup by boiling rapidly until it thickens slightly—2 to 3 minutes. Set it aside.

When the lamb is cooked, carefully transfer it to a large, hot serving platter. Cover it with foil and allow to rest in a warm place for about 20 minutes.

Meanwhile, make the plum sauce. Set a nylon sieve over a non-reactive saucepan and pour the juices from the roasting pan into it. Using a wooden spoon, press the halved plums through the sieve into the sauce pan. Stir the chicken stock into the plum mixture and season it with the remaining salt and some black pepper. Heat the sauce through, then pour it into a warm sauce boat.

Garnish the roast lamb with the plums and apple rings, and brush the fruit slices with the syrup. Serve with the plum sauce.

EDITOR'S NOTE: The long saddle of lamb comprises the loin and chump.

Rack of Lamb with a Spiced Parsley Crust

Serves 6

Working time: about 30 minutes

Total time: about 4 hours and 45 minutes
(includes marinating)

Calories 260, Protein 30g, Cholesterol 75mg, Total fat 8g,
Saturated fat 4g, Sodium 200mg

2	750 g (1¹/₂ lb) racks of lamb, each with six cutlets, chine bones removed, bone trips shortened by 5 cm (2 inches), trimmed of fat and prepared for roasting
1	small onion, finely chopped
2	garlic cloves. crushed
15 g/¹/₂ oz	parsley, finely chopped
¹/₄ tsp	ground cumin
¹/₄ tsp	paprika
¹/₂ tsp	salt
	freshly ground black pepper
1 tsp	saffron threads, soaked in 1 tsp boiling water for 1 hour
15 cl/¹/₄ pint	white wine
1 tsp	cornflour

In a small bowl, thoroughly mix together the onion, garlic, parsley, cumin, paprika, half the salt and some pepper. Stir in the saffron and its soaking liquid. Spread this mixture over the outer, fleshy side of the racks and leave them to marinate in a cool place, loosely covered, for 4 to 6 hours.

Preheat the oven to 220°C (425°F or Mark 7). Place the meat on a rack in a roasting pan, marinated side upwards. Roast for 25 minutes, then add the wine and 15 cl (¹/₄ pint) of water to the roasting pan and return the meat to the oven until the crusts are turning dark round the edges—about 20 minutes. (The meat will still be slightly pink in the centre, cover the racks with foil and roast them for a further 15 minutes if you like your lamb more thoroughly cooked.)

When the meat is cooked, transfer it to a warmed plate. Skim off the fat from the cooking liquid, and boil the liquid rapidly to reduce it slightly. Mix the cornflour with 1 tablespoon of water and stir it into the pan. Continue cooking over medium heat until the gravy thickens—2 to 3 minutes. Season the gravy with the remaining salt and some black pepper, and pour it into a warmed gravy boat. Slice the racks into cutlets and serve them with the gravy.

Guard of Honour

Serves 7

Working time: about 35 minutes

Total time: about 1 hour and 35 minutes

Calories 220, Protein 28g, Cholesterol 75mg, Total fat 9g,
Saturated fat 3g, Sodium 125mg

2	*850 g/(1³/4 lb) racks of lamb, each with seven cutlets, chine bones removed, bone tips shortened by 5 cm (2 inches), trimmed of fat and prepared for roasting*
1	*garlic clove, halved*
	freshly ground black pepper
1 tbsp	*tahini*
1 tbsp	*Dijon mustard*
1 tbsp	*clear honey*
1 tbsp	*mustard seeds*
1¹/2 tbsp	*sesame seeds*
1 tbsp	*finely chopped fresh tarragon, or 1 tsp dried tarragon*

Red wine gravy

12.5 cl/4 fl oz	*red wine*
15 cl/¹/4 pint	*unsalted chicken or brown stock or water*
1	*sprig fresh tarragon, or ¹/4 tsp dried tarragon*
¹/2 tsp	*clear honey*
¹/4 tsp	*salt*

Rub the garlic clove all over the flesh and bones, and
season the meat generously with black pepper.

Mix together the tahini, mustard, honey, mustard
seeds and sesame seeds. Combine 2 teaspoons of
this paste with the chopped tarragon and spread the
mixture over the concave inside of the racks.

Preheat the oven to 230°C (450°F or Mark 8). Assemble the guard by interlocking the exposed rib bone
tips. Using string, tie the racks. To prevent charring
during cooking, cover the exposed bone tips with a
single layer of aluminium foil, pressing the foil round
the bones.

Spread the remaining tahini-mustard paste over the
outside surface of the assembled guard. Place the meat
in a roasting pan.

Roast the lamb for 50 minutes to 1 hour and 10 minutes for rare to medium meat. Transfer the guard to a
warm platter, cut away the strings, and set it aside to
rest in a warm place.

To make the gravy, skim off the fat from the liquid in
the roasting pan and transfer the pan to the stove top.
Add the wine and boil it over high heat, stirring to scrape
up any sediment from the bottom of the pan. Add the
stock, tarragon, honey and salt and boil to reduce the
liquid by about half. Strain the gravy into a sauce boat.
Carve the guard at the table.

*EDITOR'S NOTE: For this recipe, ask your butcher for
matching racks—ideally from the same animal.*

Forming a Guard of Honour

INTERLOCKING THE BONE TIPS. Stand up two racks, their concave sides facing each other. Press the racks together so that the tips of the bones are interlaced.

TYING THE RACKS TOGETHER. Cut three lengths of string, each about 45 cm (18 inches) long. Tie each length round the racks. Cut another piece of string—about 75 cm (30 inches) long—and weave it in and out of the crossed ribs (above) from one end to the other. Bring the ends of the string back along the outside of the crossed ribs and tie them in a knot.

Chops Stuffed with Walnuts and Parsley

Serves 4

Working time: about 20 minutes

Total time: about 40 minutes

Calories 280, Protein 23g, Cholesterol 65mg,
Total fat 14g, Saturated fat 5g, Sodium 215mg

4	loin chops (about 125 g/4 oz each), trimmed of fat
2 tsp	safflower oil
1	onion, chopped
12.5 cl/4 fl oz	unsalted chicken stock
3 tbsp	currants
45 g/1¹/₂ oz	fresh breadcrumbs
2 tsp	chopped parsley
2 tbsp	finely chopped shelled walnuts
1 tsp	chopped fresh thyme, or ¹/₄ tsp dried thyme
¹/₄ tsp	salt
	freshly ground black pepper

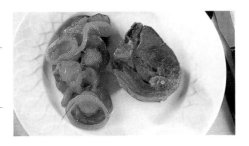

First prepare the stuffing. Heat 1 teaspoon of the oil in a non-stick frying pan over medium heat. Add the onion and cook it until it is translucent—2 to 3 minutes. Add the stock and currants and bring the liquid to a simmer. Remove the pan from the heat and cover it. Let the mixture stand until the currants have plumped up—about 5 minutes. Stir in the breadcrumbs, parsley, walnuts, thyme, ¹/₈ teaspoon of the salt and some pepper and set the stuffing aside.

Preheat the oven to 200°C (400°F or Mark 6). Arrange the chops in front of you with the fillet on the right and the apron farthest from you. Insert a small, sharp knife horizontally into each chop in turn on the right-hand side, near the end of the bone that divides the fillet from the eye. Extend the cut towards the eye, but make sure that the knife does not emerge on the far side of the eye. Rotate the knife to create a pocket within the flesh of the eye. Using a spoon or your fingers, fill the pockets with the stuffing mixture. Fold the long, thin apron of the chop to cover the opening of the pocket, and secure the apron to the fillet with a cocktail stick.

Heat the remaining teaspoon of oil in a shallow fireproof casserole over medium-high heat. Place the stuffed chops in the oil and lightly brown them on one side—1 to 2 minutes. Turn the chops over and season them with the remaining ¹/₈ teaspoon of salt and some more pepper. Put the casserole into the oven and bake the chops for 15 to 20 minutes.

Remove the casserole from the oven and let the chops rest in a warm place for 5 minutes. Remove the cocktail sticks before serving.

Crown Roast Garnished with Glazed Onions

Serves 7

Working time: about 1 hour

Total time: about 2 hours

Calories 290, Protein 29g, Cholesterol 75mg,
Total fat 14g, Saturated fat 6g, Sodium 265mg

2	850 g (1³/₄ lb) racks of lamb, each with seven cutlets, chine bones removed, bone tips shortened by 5 cm (2 inches), trimmed of fat and prepared for roasting
¹/₄ tsp	salt
	freshly ground black pepper
¹/₂ tbsp	virgin olive oil
1 tbsp	caster sugar
18	pickling onions, peeled
6 tbsp	unsalted chicken stock

Asparagus stuffing

500 g/1 lb	asparagus, washed, trimmed and peeled
1 tbsp	virgin olive oil
1	onion, finely chopped
1	garlic clove, crushed
90 g/3 oz	fresh white breadcrumbs
2 tbsp	chopped parsley
1 tsp	finely grated lemon rind
1	egg white
¹/₄ tsp	salt
	freshly ground black pepper

Assemble the racks for a crown roast. To prevent charring during cooking, cover the exposed bone tips with a single layer of aluminium foil, pressing the foil round the bones. Season the crown with the salt and some pepper; place it in a roasting pan. Preheat the oven to 220°C (425°F or Mark 7).

To make the stuffing, cut off the asparagus tips and set them aside. Cut the stems into thin slices and blanch them in boiling water for 1 minute. Using a slotted spoon, remove the slices to a colander to drain well, then set them aside. Add the asparagus tips to the water and cook them until they are tender—2 to 3 minutes. Pour them into a colander and refresh them under cold running water. Drain the tips and set them aside.

Heat the oil for the stuffing in a heavy frying pan over medium heat. Add the chopped onion, then reduce the heat to low and cook until the onion is soft but not brown—6 to 8 minutes. Add the garlic and asparagus stems to the pan and cook for a further 3 minutes. Remove the pan from the heat and stir in the breadcrumbs, parsley, lemon rind and egg white. Season the stuffing with the salt and some pepper and squeeze it gently together.

Fill the centre of the crown with the stuffing. Roast the crown for 10 minutes, then reduce the oven temperature to 180°C (350°F or Mark 4) and continue roasting for 50 to 60 minutes for rare to medium meat.

Fifteen minutes before the crown is ready, prepare the garnish. Heat the oil in a frying pan over moderate heat and sprinkle in the sugar. Heat until the sugar turns to a golden caramel. Add the onions and shake the pan gently until they are evenly coated with the caramel. Reduce the heat to low, add the stock and cover the pan. Cook until the onions are nearly tender—about 8 minutes—then add the asparagus tips. Cook for a further 2 to 3 minutes, until the onions are soft and the asparagus is heated through.

Place the crown on a warm serving dish, and garnish it with the glazed onions and asparagus tips.

Chilled Cutlets Coated with Mint Aspic

Serves 6

Working time: about 1 hour and 15 minutes
Total time: about 4 hours and 30 minutes
(includes cooling and setting)
Calories 255, Protein 35g, Cholesterol 75mg,
Total fat 12g, Saturated fat 6g, Sodium 230mg

2	750 g (1$^1/_2$ lb) racks of lamb, each with six cutlets, chined, bone tips shortened by 5 cm (2 inches)
$^1/_2$ tsp	salt
	shredded lettuce, for garnish
12	spring onions, cut into brushes, for garnish

Mint aspic

90 cl/1$^1/_2$ pints	unsalted chicken stock
3	eggs, whites and shells only
45 g/1$^1/_2$ oz	powdered gelatine
2 tbsp	red wine vinegar
4 tbsp	chopped mint

Preheat the oven to 220°C (425°F or Mark 7). Prepare the racks for roasting, and sprinkle them with the salt. Place the racks in a roasting pan and roast them for 10 minutes, then reduce the oven temperature to 180°C (350°F or Mark 4) and continue roasting for a further 30 to 40 minutes for rare to medium meat. Transfer the lamb to a large plate and allow it to cool for 1 hour, then refrigerate it for about 1 hour, until chilled.

Meanwhile, prepare the aspic. Put a large piece of muslin, a wire balloon whisk and a large metal sieve into a large saucepan. Fill the saucepan with cold water and bring it to the boil to scald the contents and the saucepan. Pour the boiling water into a large mixing bowl, to scald that also, then pour the water away.

Wring out the muslin. Line the sieve with the muslin and place it over the mixing bowl.

Put the stock into the saucepan and add the egg whites, egg shells, gelatine and vinegar. Place the saucepan over a medium heat and bring the mixture to the boil, whisking with the balloon whisk until a thick foam forms on the surface. Stop whisking and allow the liquid to boil until the foam rises to the top of the saucepan. At once, remove the saucepan from the heat and allow the foam to settle back down in the saucepan. Repeat this process twice more, without whisking, then remove the saucepan from the heat and allow it to stand for 10 minutes. Carefully pour the liquid into the muslin-lined sieve, without allowing the foam to break up. When the liquid has completely drained through, discard the foam. Allow the aspic to cool for about 1 hour, then stir in the mint.

Remove the chine bones from the lamb. Cut down between the ribs to divide each rack into six cutlets. Carefully cut away all the excess fat to leave just the lean eye of the meat attached to the bone. Place the cutlets on a wire rack set over a large clean tray.

Stir the aspic over ice, or refrigerate it, until it begins to thicken. Spoon aspic over each cutlet to coat it evenly. Refrigerate the cutlets for 10 to 15 minutes, until the aspic has set, then coat them once again. Refrigerate them until the aspic is firmly set—about 20 minutes.

Arrange the cutlets on a bed of shredded lettuce. Serve garnished with the spring onion brushes.

EDITOR'S NOTE: To make spring onion brushes, trim off the bulb and onion top to leave a 7.5 cm (3 inch) length of firm stalk. Make three or four 2.5 cm (1 inch) long cuts into each end of each onion. Place the spring onions in iced water for about 1 hour, until the ends curl.

The cutlets may be prepared up to 24 hours in advance and kept in a covered container in the refrigerator.

Lamb with Hazelnut Sauce

Serves 6

Working (and total) time: about 30 minutes

Calories 175, Protein 23g, Cholesterol 65mg,
Total fat 14g, Saturated fat 5g, Sodium 200mg

2	*racks of lamb (about 600 g/1¼ lb each), boned, the fatty flap of meat that extends from the eye removed*
45 cl/¾ pint	*unsalted brown or chicken stock*
12.5 cl/4 fl oz	*dry white wine*
½ tsp	*salt*
	freshly ground black pepper
175 g/6 oz	*turnips, peeled and finely diced*
60 g/2 oz	*shelled hazelnuts, toasted and chopped*

Preheat the oven to 230°C (450°F or Mark 8).

To make the sauce put the stock and wine in a saucepan and boil rapidly until only half of the liquid remains—8 to 10 minutes. Season with ¼ teaspoon of the salt and some black pepper. Add the turnips to the reduced stock and simmer them until they are just tender—about 5 minutes—then remove the pan from the heat and set it aside.

While the sauce is cooking, brush a heavy frying pan with a little oil. Set the pan over high heat, then quickly seal the meat and transfer it to a roasting pan. Season the meat with the remaining salt and some black pepper. Roast the lamb for 5 to 10 minutes for rare to medium meat.

Just before the meat is ready, return the sauce to the heat. Stir in the chopped hazelnuts and heat the sauce through.

Carve the lamb and arrange slices on six plates. Serve with the sauce spooned over the meat.

EDITOR'S NOTE: To toast hazelnuts, put them on a baking sheet in a preheated 130°C (350°F or Mark 4) oven for 10 minutes.

Loin with Juniper Berry Sauce

Serves 8

Working time: about 20 minutes

Total time: about 30 minutes

Calories 250, Protein 25g, Cholesterol 90mg,
Total fat 12g, Saturated fat 5g, Sodium 70mg

2	*loins of lamb (about 1 kg/2¼ lb each), boned and trimmed of fat, fillet reserved for another recipe*
1 litre/1¾ pints	*unsalted brown or chicken stock*
30 cl/½ pint	*dry Madeira*
4 tsp	*redcurrant jelly*
4 tsp	*juniper berries, coarsely crushed with a pestle and mortar*
1 tsp	*virgin olive oil*

Preheat the oven to 220°C (425°F or Mark 7).

Put the stock, Madeira and redcurrant jelly in a heavy-bottomed saucepan and boil them over high heat until the liquid is reduced to about ½ litre (16 fl oz). Add half the juniper berries and continue boiling until the stock has further reduced to about 30 cl (½ pint), then remove the pan from the heat and set it aside.

Meanwhile, brush the eyes of loin with the oil, sprinkle the meat with the remaining juniper berries and place it in a roasting pan. Roast the meat on the middle shelf of the oven for 12 minutes. Turn off the heat and leave the lamb in the pan on the floor of the oven for 10 minutes.

Transfer the lamb to a warmed serving dish, cover the dish and set it aside in a warm place. Skim off any fat from the juices in the pan and pour the remaining juices into the juniper berry sauce. Reheat the sauce, pour some of it round the lamb to moisten it and pour the rest into a warmed sauce boat. Serve immediately.

Loin Stuffed with Wild Mushrooms

Serves 4

Working time: about 1 hour

Total time: about 2 hours

Calories 235, Protein 24g, Cholesterol 175mg,
Total fat 12g, Saturated fat 4g, Sodium 225mg

1 kg/2¹/₄ lb	*loin, boned and trimmed of fat eye only*
30 g/1 oz	*dried wild mushrooms (chanterelle, ceps or shiitake), soaked for 20 minutes in hot water*
1 tbsp	*virgin olive oil*
3	*spring onions, white parts finely chopped, green tops cut into 2.5 cm (1 inch) pieces*
1 tbsp	*finely chopped celery*
2	*garlic cloves, finely chopped*
2 tsp	*fresh thyme, or ³/₄ tsp dried thyme*
125 g/4 oz	*fresh mushrooms, wiped clean and chopped*
¹/₄ litre/8 fl oz	*unsalted brown stock*
1 tbsp	*fresh lemon juice*
¹/₄ tsp	*salt*
	freshly ground black pepper

Remove the dried mushrooms from their soaking liquid; cut off and discard any woody or sandy stems. Finely chop the mushrooms and set them aside. Carefully strain the mushroom-soaking liquid through a muslin-lined sieve set over a bowl to remove any grit. Set the bowl aside.

Heat half of the oil in a heavy-bottomed saucepan over medium heat. Add the white parts of the spring onions, the celery, garlic and half of the thyme. Cook the mixture, stirring occasionally, for 3 minutes. Add the reconstituted dried mushrooms and fresh mushrooms to the pan together with 4 tablespoons of the stock, the lemon juice, half of the salt and a generous grinding of pepper. Cover the pan, reduce the heat to low, and cook the mushrooms, stirring them every now and then, until all the liquid has been absorbed—20 to 25 minutes. Transfer the mushroom stuffing to a bowl and let it cool to room temperature.

Preheat the oven to 220°C (425°F or Mark 7). To butterfly the eye of loin and prepare it for stuffing, cut it in half horizontally, leaving the halves hinged at one side. Open out the meat and spread the stuffing down the centre. Fold the halves back together and tie the meat securely. Place the meat in a heavy roasting pan and brush it with the remaining oil. Roast the lamb for about 25 minutes for medium meat.

Remove the pan from the oven and set the lamb aside on a carving board while you prepare the sauce. Skim off the fat from the pan, leaving behind any caramelized juices. Place the pan over medium heat. Pour the strained mushroom liquid and the remaining stock into the pan, stirring well with a wooden spoon to dissolve the caramelized juices in the bottom. Stir in the remaining salt, the remaining thyme, the green spring onion tops and some pepper. Boil the liquid until about 12.5 cl (4 fl oz) of sauce remains—about 10 minutes.

Cut the lamb into 12 slices and arrange them on a serving dish or on individual plates. Pour the sauce over the slices and serve immediately.

EDITOR'S NOTE: Only the eye of the loin is used here; reserve the fillet for another recipe where lean meat is called for.

Loin on a Bed of Green Leaves

Ask the butcher to saw through the chine bone of the loins
to make it easier to carve the meat.

Serves 8

Working t me: about 40 minutes
Total time: about 1 hour and 45 minutes
Calories 235, Protein 24g, Cholesterol 75mg,
Total fat 12g, Saturated fat 4g, Sodium 195mg

2	*loins (about 1 kg/2 ¹/₄ lb each), trimmed of fat*
1 tbsp	*virgin olive oil*
1 tbsp	*grainy mustard*
¹/₈ tsp	*salt*
	freshly ground black pepper
2	*garlic cloves, finely chopped*
25 g/³/₄ oz	*fresh wholemeal breadcrumbs*
1 tbsp	*chopped parsley*
1 tsp	*chopped fresh thyme, or ¹/₄ tsp dried thyme*
1 tsp	*chopped fresh rosemary, or ¹/₄ tsp dried rosemary, crumbled*

Wilted green leaf salad

1 tbsp	*virgin olive oil*
2	*spring onions, trimmed and chopped*
500 g/1 lb	*dandelion greens or spinach, stemmed, washed and dried*
1	*bunch watercress, trimmed, washed and dried*
16	*cherry tomatoes, halved*
1 tbsp	*red wine vinegar*
¹/₈ tsp	*salt*
	freshly ground black pepper

Put the lamb in a roasting pan bone side down. In a small bowl, combine 1 teaspoon of the oil, the mustard, salt, some pepper and half of the garlic. Rub this mixture over the lamb and let it stand at room temperature for 1 hour.

Preheat the oven to 220°C (425°F or Mark 7). Roast the lamb until it has browned—25 to 35 minutes for rare to medium meat.

Mix together the breadcrumbs, parsley, thyme, rosemary, the remaining garlic and some pepper. Sprinkle the breadcrumb mixture over the top of the lamb; dribble the remaining 2 teaspoons of oil over the breadcrumbs. Continue roasting the lamb until the breadcrumbs have browned—about 10 minutes more. Keep the lamb warm while you make the salad.

For the salad, heat the oil in a heavy frying pan or sauté pan over medium-high heat. Add the spring onions and sauté them for 45 seconds, then add the greens, watercress, tomatoes and vinegar. Toss the vegetables until the greens are slightly wilted—about 30 seconds. Remove the pan from the heat and season the salad with the salt and some pepper.

Carve the lamb into 16 pieces and serve them on beds of salad.

Moroccan Spiced Stew

Serves 4
Working time: about 30 minutes
Total time: about 1 hour and 45 minutes
Calories 315, Protein 36g, Cholesterol 80mg,
Total fat 14g, Saturated fat 4g, Sodium 175mg

500 g/1 lb	*lean lamb (from the leg), trimmed of fat and cut into 2.5 cm (1 inch) cubes*
1/2 tsp	*safflower oil*
350 g/12 oz	*pickling onions*
45 cl/3/4 pint	*unsalted brown or chicken stock*
1 tbsp	*clear honey*
1 tsp	*ground cinnamon*
1/2 tsp	*saffron threads*
1/2 tsp	*ground ginger*
1/4 tsp	*grated nutmeg*
1/2	*orange, grated rind and juice*
12	*ready-to-eat stoned prunes*
30 g/1 oz	*blanched almonds*
1/4 tsp	*salt*
	freshly ground black pepper

Heat the oil in a non-stick frying pan over medium-high heat and sauté the onions until they are golden-brown—about 5 minutes. Transfer them to a bowl and set them aside.

Add the lamb cubes to the frying pan and brown them for 2 to 3 minutes. Transfer them to a large heavy-bottomed saucepan or fireproof casserole.

Pour off any fat from the frying pan, then add the stock and bring it to the boil, stirring with a wooden spoon to dislodge any deposits from the bottom of the pan. Pour the boiling stock over the lamb. Add the honey, cinnamon, saffron, ginger and nutmeg to the casserole, cover and simmer for 30 minutes.

Add the onions, orange rind and juice to the lamb and simmer for a further 30 minutes. Finally add the prunes, almonds and salt, season with pepper and simmer, uncovered, for 15 minutes.

EDITOR'S NOTE: The prunes used in this recipe are sold for eating straight from the packet and do not require presoaking or stoning. If you use ordinary dried prunes, soak them in cold water for 3 hours and stone them before cooking.

Braised Lamb with Mango

Serves 4
Working time: about 30 minutes
Total time: about 7 hours and 30 minutes
(includes marinating)
Calories 300, Protein 45g, Cholesterol 75mg,
Total fat 10g, Saturated fat 4g, Sodium 320mg

500 g/1 lb	lamb slices, cut from the fillet end of the leg, trimmed of fat and cut into 7.5 cm (3 inch) long strips
30 cl/¹/₂ pint	plain low-fat yoghurt
1 tsp	finely chopped fresh ginger root
1 tbsp	ground coriander
1 tsp	ground cumin
2 tsp	safflower oil
1	onion, finely sliced
1	garlic clove, crushed
2 tsp	coriander seeds, crushed
1 tbsp	cornflour
2.5 cl/4 fl oz	unsalted chicken stock
1	bay leaf
¹/₈ tsp	powdered saffron or turmeric
³/₄ tsp	salt
2	mangoes
4	large fresh coriander leaves

Mix together the yoghurt, ginger, ground coriander and cumin, then stir in the strips of lamb, coating them in the mixture. Cover the meat and leave it to marinate in the refrigerator for at least 6 hours, or overnight.

In a heavy-bottomed fireproof casserole, heat the oil and stir in the onion and garlic. Cook them over low heat for 1 minute, then add the crushed coriander seeds and sauté until the seeds begin to pop. Mix the cornflour with a tablespoon of the lamb marinade. Stir the cornflour mixture into the rest of the marinade. Transfer the meat and its marinade to the casserole and continue cooking gently for 1 minute. Add the stock, bay leaf, saffron or turmeric, and salt. Cover the casserole and simmer the stew over low heat until the meat is tender—about 1 hour.

Peel the mangoes; cut two thin slices from one of them and reserve these for a garnish. Remove the stones and cut the flesh into 1 cm (¹/₂ inch) cubes. Add the mango cubes to the lamb and simmer the casserole over low heat for a further 5 minutes.

Just before serving, coarsely chop the coriander leaves and sprinkle them over the lamb. Serve it garnished with the reserved slices of mango.

Lamb Dhansak

Serves 4

Working time: about 50 minutes

Total time: about 10 hours (includes soaking)

Calories 285, Protein 35g, Cholesterol 75mg, Total fat 8g,
Saturated fat 4g, Sodium 340mg

500 g/1 lb	*lean lamb (from the leg), trimmed of fat and cut into 2.5 cm (1 inch) cubes*
1	*large onion, finely chopped*
2 tsp	*ground coriander*
2 tsp	*ground cumin*
1 tsp	*ground cinnamon*
1 tsp	*ground cardamom*
1 tsp	*ground turmeric*
1 tsp	*black peppercorns*
20 cl/7 fl oz	*plain low-fat yoghurt*
2	*garlic cloves, crushed*
2	*fresh hot green chili peppers, finely chopped*
2.5 cm/1 inch	*piece fresh ginger root, finely chopped*
250 g/8 oz	*mixed lentils, washed, soaked for 8 hours or overnight, drained*
350 g/12 oz	*aubergine, trimmed and cut into 2 .5 cm (1 inch) cubes*
250 g/8 oz	*butternut squash, peeled and cut into 2.5 cm (1 inch) cubes*
350 g/12 oz	*tomatoes, finely chopped*
150 g/5 oz	*fresh spinach, thoroughly washed and torn into small pieces*
1/2 tsp	*salt*
3 tbsp	*finely chopped fresh coriander*

Brush a large fireproof casserole or heavy-bottomed saucepan with oil. Add the onion and cook it over medium-high heat, stirring constantly, until it is softened—about 2 to 3 minutes. Stir in the lamb, ground coriander, cumin, cinnamon, cardamom, turmeric and peppercorns, then add 1 tablespoon of the yoghurt. Cook over high heat, turning the meat until the yoghurt is completely absorbed—3 to 5 minutes. Add the rest of the yoghurt, 1 tablespoon at a time, stirring constantly after each addition until all of the yoghurt is absorbed.

Stir in the garlic, chopped chili peppers and ginger and cook for a further 1 minute. Add the lentils, aubergine, squash, tomatoes and spinach and pour in just enough water to cover the ingredients. Bring the mixture to the boil, then reduce the heat to low, cover and simmer until the lamb is tender—about 1 hour. Check the pan from time to time and add a little more water if the stew becomes dry. About 10 minutes before the end of cooking, add the salt and 2 tablespoons of the fresh coriander.

Lift out the meat and about half of the vegetable and lentil mixture with a slotted spoon and set it aside. Using a potato masher, mash the lentil and vegetable mixture left in the pan, then reincorporate the meat and the rest of the lentil and vegetable mixture and gently reheat it. Serve garnished with the remaining tablespoon of coriander.

EDITOR'S NOTE: Oriental food shops generally stock several varieties of lentils. The mixture suggested for this recipe is channa dal, toor dal and masoor dal, but other varieties can be used instead.

Lamb with Puréed Asparagus and Jerusalem Artichokes

Serves 6

Working time: about 1 hour

Total time: about 2 hours and 30 minutes

Calories 225, Protein 30g, Cholesterol 80mg, Total fat 9g, Saturated fat 4g, Sodium 270mg

750 g/1¹/₂ lb	lean lamb (from the leg or loin), trimmed of fat and cut into 7.5 cm (3 inch) strips
500 g/1 lb	asparagus, trimmed and peeled
1 tsp	salt
¹/₂ tbsp	safflower oil
3	shallots, halved
500 g	Jerusalem artichokes
4 tsp	fresh lemon juice
60 g/2 oz	watercress, washed, trimmed, blanched for 30 seconds and chopped
¹/₄ tsp	white pepper
3 tbsp	thick Greek yoghurt

Cut off the tips of the asparagus spears and set them aside. Cook the stems in boiling water to cover, with half a teaspoon of the salt, until they are soft—about 5 minutes. Remove the stems with a slotted spoon, drain them and set them aside; strain and reserve the cooking liquid

While the asparagus is cooking, heat the oil in a frying pan, add the shallots and soften them over a me-

dium heat—about 5 minutes. Transfer the shallots to a fireproof casserole. Increase the heat under the frying pan and lightly brown the lamb strips in two batches, transferring each batch to the casserole. Pour the reserved asparagus cooking liquid over the meat and shallots. The liquid should cover the lamb; if necessary, add extra water. Simmer the casserole until the meat is tender—about 1 hour.

Meanwhile, cook the artichokes. Put 1 teaspoon of the lemon juice into a non-reactive pan with 1 litre (1³/₄ pints) of water. Peel and chop the artichokes, dropping them into the water immediately to prevent discoloration. Bring the water to the boil and cook the artichokes until tender—20 to 30 minutes. Drain the artichokes and purée them in a blender. Purée and sieve the asparagus stems. Set the purées aside.

Skim off any fat from the casserole and remove the meat and shallots. Bring the liquid in the casserole to the boil, then add the asparagus tips and cook gently until they are just tender—about 5 minutes. Remove the tips with a slotted spoon and keep them warm.

Stir the asparagus and artichoke purées and the watercress into the cooking liquid to make a sauce. Gently heat the sauce and season it with the remaining lemon juice and salt and the white pepper. Return the meat to the sauce and heat it through gently. Add the asparagus tips and swirl the yoghurt on the top. Serve at once.

Indian Lamb with Spinach

Serves 6

Working time: about 50 minutes

Total time: about 2 hours

Calories 275, Protein 37g, Cholesterol 75mg, Total fat 9g,
Saturated fat 4g, Sodium 400mg

500 g/1 lb	*lean lamb (from the leg), trimmed of fat and cut into 2.5 cm (1 inch) cubes*
1	*large onion, finely chopped*
4 tsp	*ground coriander*
1 tbsp	*mustard seeds*
2 tsp	*ground cumin*
1 tsp	*chilli powder*
1 tsp	*ground turmeric*
20 cl/7 fl oz	*plain low fat yoghurt*
2.5 cm/1 inch	*piece, fresh ginger root finely chopped*
3	*garlic cloves, crushed*
1 kg/2 lb	*fresh spinach, trimmed, thoroughly washed and torn into small pieces*
1/4 tsp	*salt*

Brush a heavy, non-stick fireproof casserole or sauce
pan with oil, add the onion and soften it over mediu
high heat for 2 to 3 minutes, stirring constantly. Stir
the lamb cubes, coriander, mustard seeds, cumin, ch
powder and turmeric and mix all the ingredients th
oughly together. Add 1 tablespoon of the yoghurt a
cook over high heat, stirring the meat continuously u
all of the yoghurt is absorbed—3 to 5 minutes. A
the rest of the yoghurt, 1 tablespoon at a time, stirri
constantly after each addition until the yoghurt is co
pletely absorbed.

Stir in the ginger and garlic, add just enough wa
to cover the meat and bring the liquid to the boil. Co
the casserole, reduce the heat and simmer until t
lamb is tender—about 1 hour.

When the meat is cooked, increase the heat
medium and add the spinach in batches, stirring ea
batch until it is wilted. When all the spinach is incorp
rated cook the stew, uncovered, over high heat
evaporate any excess liquid—about 5 minutes. A
the salt just before serving.

Lamb and Apple Casserole

Serves 4

Working time: about 30 minutes

Total time: about 2 hours and 25 minutes

Calories 430, Protein 40g, Cholesterol 75mg,
Total fat 10g, Saturated fat 5g, Sodium 290mg

500 g/1 lb	*lean lamb (from the loin), trimmed of fat and cut into thin slices*
50 g/1¹/₂ lb	*potatoes, very thinly sliced*
2 tsp	*finely chopped fresh sage, or ¹/₂ tsp dried sage*
1	*orange, finely grated rind and juice*
¹/₂ tsp	*salt*
	freshly ground black pepper
0 g/1¹/₄ lb	*dessert apples, peeled, cored and sliced*
1	*large onion, sliced into very thin rings*
5 cl/¹/₄ pint	*dry cider*

eheat the oven to 180°C (350°F or Mark 4). Arrange
f of the potato slices in the bottom of a 2.5 litre (4
t) casserole. Sprinkle them with a little of the sage,
ange rind and salt, and plenty of black pepper.

Cover the potatoes with half the apple slices; season this layer in the same way.

Continue to build up the casserole in layers as fol-
lows, seasoning each layer with some of the sage,
orange rind, salt and pepper. Arrange the slices of lamb
evenly over the apple, and spread the onion rings over
the lamb, leaving a small space uncovered in the centre of the layer. Cover the onion with the remaining
apples, and top the casserole with the remaining potatoes, maintaining the small gap in the centre of both
layers and overlapping the slices of potato on the top
layer in neat concentric circles.

Mix the orange juice and cider together and pour
the liquid slowly into the hole in the centre of the potato topping. Cover and cook the casserole in the oven
for 1¹/₂ hours, then remove the lid and continue cooking until the ingredients feel tender when pierced with
a fine skewer and the potato topping is golden-brown—
30 to 45 minutes. Serve the casserole hot, straight
from the dish.

Navarin with Mustard Croûtons

Serves 4

Working time: about 45 minutes

Total time: about 7 hours (includes chilling)

Calories 430, Protein 35g, Cholesterol 75mg, Total fat 9g,
Saturated fat 4g, Sodium 600mg

500 g/1 lb	*lean stewing lamb, trimmed of fat and cut into 2 cm (³/₄ inch) cubes*
1 tbsp	*plain flour*
60 cl/1 pint	*unsalted brown or chicken stock*
1	*onion, sliced*
2 tbsp	*tomato paste*
2	*fresh bay leaves*
1 tsp	*chopped fresh thyme, or ¹/₄ tsp dried thyme*
¹/₄ tsp	*salt*
	freshly ground black pepper
250 g/8 oz	*turnips, peeled*
250 g/8 oz	*tiny new potatoes, scrubbed*
250 g/8 oz	*courgettes*
250 g/8 oz	*cherry tomatoes, skinned, or large tomatoes, skinned and quartered*
1	*small baguette (about 35 cm/14 inches long)*
2	*garlic cloves*
4 tsp	*grainy mustard*

Preheat the oven to 190°C (375°F or Mark 5). Toss ■ meat in the flour. Heat a fireproof casserole over a h■ heat and add the meat, stirring until the cubes ■ seared on all sides. Stir in the stock, onion, toma■ paste, bay leaves, thyme, salt and some pepper. Br■ the mixture to the boil. Cover the casserole, transfe■ to the oven and cook it for 50 minutes.

Cut the turnips into 2.5 cm (1 inch) pieces, then u■ a potato peeler to pare down their sharp edges, giv■ the pieces an attractive rounded shape. Add the t■ nips and potatoes to the casserole and return it to ■ oven for a further 50 minutes. Remove the casser■ from the oven, allow the stew to cool, then transfe■ to a bowl and refrigerate it until a layer of fat forms the surface—4 hours or overnight.

Preheat the oven to 190°C (375°F or Mark 5). L■ off and discard the layer of fat, remove the bay leav■ and transfer the stew to a clean casserole. Prepa■ the courgettes in the same way as the turnips and s■ them into the casserole with the tomatoes. Cut t■ baguette diagonally into 1 cm (¹/₂ inch) slices. Halve ■ cloves of garlic and rub their cut surfaces all over the bre■ Spread one side of the bread slices with mustard a■ arrange them, mustard side up, around the edge of ■ casserole. Cook the navarin, uncovered, until it is heat■ through and the bread is crisp—about 25 minutes.